Immanuel Kant

To Perpetual Peace

A Philosophical Sketch

TRANSLATED, WITH INTRODUCTION,
by Ted Humphrey

Hackett Publishing Company, Inc.
Indianapolis/Cambridge

Copyright © 2003 by Hackett Publishing Company, Inc.

21 20 19 18   3 4 5 6 7

For further information, please address:
    Hackett Publishing Company, Inc.
    P.O. Box 44937
    Indianapolis, IN 46244-0937

    www.hackettpublishing.com

Cover design by Listenberger Design & Associates
Interior design by Abigail Coyle
Composition by Jennifer Plumley

Library of Congress Cataloging-in-Publication Data
Kant, Immanuel, 1724–1804.
    [Zum ewigen Frieden. English.]
    To perpetual peace: a philosophical sketch/Immanuel Kant;
translated, with introduction, by Ted Humphrey.
    p. cm.
Includes bibliographical references.
    ISBN 0-87220-692-0 — ISBN 0-87220-691-2 (pbk.)
    1. International law. 2. Peace. 3. International organization.
I. Humphrey, Ted, 1941– II. Title.

KZ2322.A3Z8613 2003
341.7'3—dc21

                                                2003047180

ISBN-13: 978-0-87220-692-2
ISBN-13: 978-0-87220-691-5 (pbk.)

Immanuel Kant

To Perpetual Peace

Contents

Translator's Introduction

To Perpetual Peace: A Philosophical Sketch is important for completing Kant's political theory and philosophy of history and for addressing yet one more seemingly intractable issue of continuing concern to humanity, the course to and prospects for peace among peoples and nations. One thus has at least two reasons for reading this work. Here Kant fills out his moral and political theory, envisioning the task of pursuing enduring peace among nations as one of the ends of moral and political action. At the same time, Kant takes stands on and asks questions about issues that are of direct, immediate concern to us all, namely the following:

- What is the standing of a sovereign nation, and what are its rights relative to other sovereign nations?
- What is our obligation to pursue peace?
- Can one justify intervening in the affairs of another sovereign nation?
- Who, if anyone, has the right to intervene?

I write this introduction just as members of the United Nations debate these very issues, seeking a way out of the latest Middle East crisis, one discussion among many, as humanity gropes toward its goal of making the world a place in which persons are free to seek their personal and social ends. Beyond its significance in Kant's political theory and philosophy of history, this book shines a light on the practice of international politics, forcing the reflective person seriously to question existing structures and strategies.

First published in 1795, *Perpetual Peace* is the last of Kant's Enlightenment essays dealing with history, human progress, the foundations of political association, and the relation between moral and prudential principles.[1] From the perspective of Kant's philosophical system, this essay is particularly important because it argues that humans are obligated to pursue a well-ordered system of relations among nations and that such a system is a necessary condition for the fulfillment of the human condition. Pessimistically but realistically recognizing the practical obstacles to creating a world system that both promotes and preserves peaceful relations among nations, Kant nonetheless optimistically and idealistically asserts that humans have the capacity and obligation to pursue strategies that will do so. Kant's argument in this regard underscores his fundamental position that what is morally obligatory always takes precedence over mere prudence and that free rational beings are able to do what they are obliged to do. Consequently, they can and must pursue peace, even under the most daunting circumstances.

Although *Perpetual Peace* is best read as Kant published it, from beginning to end, the doctrine of "publicity" that Kant articulates in the tract's final section underpins the argument and course of action he advocates. Throughout the essay, Kant has argued that moral principles must govern our action in the international as well as the national and personal arenas. Just as he has earlier provided formulae by which we determine whether actions conform with duty in the personal sphere, here he propounds a formula for use in determining whether in the international sphere a course of action conforms with duty. This he calls the *transcendental formula* of public right:

> "All actions that affect the rights of other men are wrong if their maxim is not consistent with publicity."

This principle is to be considered not only *ethical* (as belonging to the doctrine of virtue), but also *juridical* (as pertaining

---

[1] Immanuel Kant, *Perpetual Peace and Other Essays on Politics, History, and Morals,* trans. Ted Humphrey, Hackett Publishing Company, Indianapolis, 1992, includes the full set of essays devoted to these topics. The introduction to that volume sets these essays in the context of Kant's philosophical system. The parenthesized page numbers in the text of this introduction refer to the marginal page numbers in this translation of *Perpetual Peace* itself.

to the rights of men). If my maxim cannot be *openly divulged* without at the same time defeating my own intention, i.e., must be kept *secret* for it to succeed, or if I cannot *publicly acknowledge* it without thereby inevitably arousing everyone's opposition to my plan, then this necessary and universal, and thus *a priori* foreseeable, opposition of all to me could not have come from anything other than the injustice with which it threatens everyone. (381)

As Kant acknowledges, the doctrine of publicity does not provide positive guidance for action, but it does provide a clear, workable criterion to warn us off from certain courses of action. What we cannot do in the clear light of day, because it would not simply be a matter of embarrassment but would predictably raise others' opposition since they would perceive it as harmful to their interests, we ought to refrain from doing. Ultimately, however, this negative doctrine of publicity is not sufficient, for it does not prevent the powerful from imposing themselves on the less powerful. Thus, Kant proceeds to a positive formulation of the doctrine of publicity, " 'All maxims that *require* publicity (in order not to fail of their end) agree with both politics and morality'." (386) This positive doctrine of publicity sets the context for all action in the personal, social, and political spheres. What we can achieve only by bringing it to light and making it a shared project for all conduces to "the universal public end (happiness)." This is the true task of politics.

Publicity is the context and goal of political life, to seek and preserve peace. In preparing to pursue this goal, Kant asserts that we must adopt certain preparatory behaviors, without doing which it would be impossible even to enter the road to peace. First, we must enter into treaties of peace not only in good faith but also with full intent, without reservations to be settled at a later time. (343–4) Such reservations can only serve as matters for subsequent dispute and thus undermine the intent to establish peace. Second, nations are by their nature autonomous, not subject to acquisition by other nations. Nations arise logically as a function of a social contract among a people who are thereby subjects and citizens, giving the nation the status of a "moral person." (344) Third, nations must abolish standing armies, as their very existence signals other nations that one is prepared for and thus disposed to war. Their very existence creates the need of other nations to protect themselves. Similarly, fourth, nations are not to incur foreign debt, which must inevitably become a cause for strife between creditor and borrower with the potential to embroil them and other nations in conflict. Nations must forgo interfering in each others' internal affairs. This fifth principle rests on the second, reaffirming each nation's status as a moral person. Finally, sixth, even at war, nations are to conduct themselves in such ways as not to undermine their credibility and the trust of those with whom they are hostilely engaged.

These are articles preliminary to perpetual peace because they constitute fundamental conditions without which it will be impossible to establish relations of trust and accord. The first, fifth, and sixth preliminary articles establish foundations of trust and respect, and ought to be adopted immediately. They are articles to which each nation can immediately and directly commit itself as a moral person, signaling its regard for the integrity of other nations. Trust and respect established, nations can and ought to give up their armies, coercive financial entanglements, and attempts at acquiring other nations as if they were mere property. Although pursuing elimination of these practices is as obligatory as adopting the former attitudes, doing so immediately is not prudentially in a given nation's interest. Kant is sufficiently realistic to acknowledge this circumstance and thus to concede that these principles be adopted over time, as trust develops. They nonetheless constitute necessary conditions for peace.

Even having adopted these preliminary articles, nations as moral persons remain in a state of nature. Emerging from the perdurant state of nature requires an explicit act. Nations must establish the civil condition among themselves. (349) The three conditions that are requisite to establishing the civil condition among nations that underlies the possibility of perpetual peace each acknowledge and ensure the integrity and autonomy of the individual person and are thus conditions in which all have a personal and collective interest. Kant regards only one form of civil constitution compatible with free moral agency. This he denominates a republican form of constitution, which by his definition acknowledges the freedom of individuals as they enter into a contract to subject themselves to a "single, common . . . legislation," whereby they are all citizens equal under the law. (349–50)

Under such civil constitutions, Kant argues, nations will hesitate to go to war, because in war all citizens equally expose themselves to risk. Further, and perhaps of more importance, the citizens of such nations will have an interest not merely in avoiding risk but also in actively furthering and ensuring their freedom and security. This interest requires nations to federate themselves for the purpose of guaranteeing their integrity and rights as nations. This federation cannot itself become a nation of nations. That outcome would compromise the original nations and thus the integrity of original citizenship. Nonetheless, the federation of nations exists as a *"league of peace"* whose goal is to end war permanently. On the one hand, such a federation curbs the natural tendency of nations to see the use of force or might as the means of asserting their sovereign right, whereas, on the other, it expresses humanity's natural drive to create the conditions of its genuine freedom. A sovereign nation's right consists of being able to pursue its citizens' legitimate ends without threatening other nations' citizens or being threatened by them. This requires mutual commitment to peace.

Ultimately, the league of peace guarantees humanity's cosmopolitan right, that is, each person's right to pursue his or her destiny in the world. Although persons may by coincidence of birth be citizens of a given nation, "the right to the *earth's surface* . . . belongs in common to the totality of men [and] makes commerce possible." (358) Cosmopolitan right underlies the very possibility of sustained human moral and material progress.

In our present condition, that is, the eternally present disposition of nations to settle their differences by contests of might, what assurance can we have that perpetual peace is possible? What motives beyond the command of duty, which binds absolutely, do we have for pursuing peace? Kant's answer to these questions derives from his systematic theory about the limits of human knowledge. First, we cannot properly be said to have knowledge that will allow us to answer these questions. Rather, perpetual peace is for humanity a moral end or goal that derives from humanity's capacities for free rational action. Perpetual peace is both the goal of free rational action and the condition under which such action is fully realizable. Nonetheless, persons are material beings in the world, and it is not immediately apparent that the world either provides for or permits the possibility of perpetual peace. Although Kant disallows knowledge of the possibility that it either does or does not—such knowledge necessarily transcends the boundaries of possible experience—we have grounds for believing that it does. Nature appears to provide for the eventuality of perpetual peace in three related ways: Humanity's state of nature requires that peoples enter into the social contract as nations. The multiplicity of nations requires a federation of peace. Finally, humanity's need and desire to seek the goods of this world that gives rise to the *"spirit of trade,"* which is incompatible with war, motivates it to seek such peace as will guarantee cosmopolitan right. (365–68)

Kant's penultimate point concerns the right of academics in particular, but also citizens in general, to express their views regarding issues that touch on matters of state, as this essay of Kant's does. In fact, Kant argues that consulting the views of academics on such matters is obligatory, if only by allowing them to express those views publicly. In this way, citizens exercise their free rationality openly, and the nation's legislative authority can at its discretion evaluate and determine whether to adopt their theories. Throughout his Enlightenment essays, particularly in *What Is Enlightenment?* and *Theory and Practice*, Kant argues that humanity's development and exercise of reason are a necessary condition of its achieving morally obligatory ends, that humanity has a duty, by virtue of its free rationality, to seek maturity and full citizenship, which in turn require the civil condition among persons and nations. We thus return to where we began: Publicity provides the only context for true civic life.

Kant's philosophical system grounds the argument of *Perpetual Peace*. Whether one finds the argument either valid or persuasive will depend on one's estimate of that vast architectonic structure, of which the essay's doctrines are important elements. That is reason enough for attending to this and the other Enlightenment essays. The ultimate reason for attending to a writer, however, is not simply to enter his or her arcane world, but to enter because it sheds light on the world in which we find ourselves. Few essays can more probingly stimulate thought about our present condition than *Perpetual Peace*.

Ted Humphrey
Tempe, Arizona

TO PERPETUAL PEACE
A PHILOSOPHICAL SKETCH[1]
(1795)

To Perpetual Peace

Whether this satirical inscription on a certain Dutch shopkeeper's sign, on which a graveyard was painted, holds for *men* in general, or especially for heads of state who can never get enough of war, or perhaps only for philosophers who dream that sweet dream, is not for us to decide. However, the author of this essay does set out one condition: The practical politician tends to look down with great smugness on the political theorist, regarding him as an academic whose empty ideas cannot endanger the nation[2] since the nation must proceed on principles [derived from] experience; consequently, the theorist is allowed to fire his entire volley, without the *worldly-wise* statesman becoming the least bit concerned. Now if he is to be consistent—and this is the condition I set out—the practical politician must not claim, in the event of a dispute with a theorist, to detect some danger to the nation in those views that the political theorist expresses openly and without ulterior motive. By this *clausula salvatoria*, the author of this essay will regard himself to be expressly protected in the best way possible from all malicious interpretation.

1

First Section
Which Contains the Preliminary Articles for Perpetual Peace Among Nations

1. No treaty of peace that tacitly reserves issues for a future war shall be held valid.

For if this were the case, it would be a mere truce, a suspension of hostilities, not *peace*, which means the end of all hostilities, so much so that even to modify it by "perpetual" smacks of pleonasm. A peace treaty nullifies all existing causes for war, even if they are unknown to the contracting parties, and even if they are assiduously ferreted out from archival documents. When one or both parties to a peace treaty, being too exhausted to continue the war, has a mental reservation (*reservatio mentalis*) concerning some presently unmentioned pretension that will be revived at the first opportune moment, since ill will between the warring parties still remains, that reservation is a bit of mere Jesuitical casuistry. If we judge such actions in their true character, they are beneath the dignity of a ruler, just as a willingness to indulge in reasoning of this sort is beneath his minister's dignity.

If, however, enlightened concepts of political prudence lead us to believe that the true honor of a nation lies in its continual increase of power by whatever means necessary, this judgment will appear academic and pedantic.

2. No independent nation, be it large or small, may be acquired by another nation by inheritance, exchange, purchase, or gift.

A nation is not (like the ground on which it is located) a possession (*patrimonium*). It is a society of men whom no other than the nation itself can command or dispose of. Since, like a tree, each nation has its own roots, to incorporate it into another nation as a graft, denies its existence as a moral person, turns it into a thing, and thus contradicts the concept of the original contract, without which a people has no rights.* Everyone is aware of the danger that this

---

*A hereditary monarch is not a nation that can be inherited by another nation; only the right to rule it can be inherited by another physical person. Consequently, the nation acquires a ruler, but the ruler as such (i.e., as one who already has another kingdom) does not acquire the nation.

purported right of acquisition by the marriage of nations to one another—a custom unknown in other parts of the world—has brought to Europe, even in the most recent times. It is a new form of industry, in which influence is increased without expending energy, and territorial possessions are extended merely by establishing family alliances. The hiring out of one nation's troops to another for use against an enemy not common to both of them falls under this principle, for by this practice subjects are used and wasted as mere objects to be manipulated at will.

3. *Standing armies* (miles perpetuus) *shall be gradually abolished.*   345

For they constantly threaten other nations with war by giving the appearance that they are prepared for it, which goads nations into competing with one another in the number of men under arms, and this practice knows no bounds. And since the costs related to maintaining peace will in this way finally become greater than those of a short war, standing armies are the cause of wars of aggression that are intended to end burdensome expenditures. Moreover, paying men to kill or be killed appears to use them as mere machines and tools in the hand of another (the nation), which is inconsistent with the rights of humanity. The voluntary, periodic military training of citizens so that they can secure their homeland against external aggression is an entirely different matter. The same could be said about the hoarding of treasure (for of the three sorts of power, the *power of an army*, the *power of alliance*, and the *power of money*, the third is the most reliable instrument of war). Thus, except for the difficulty in discovering the amount of wealth another nation possesses, the hoarding of treasure could be regarded as preparation for war that necessitates aggression.

4. *No national debt shall be contracted in connection with the foreign affairs of the nation.*

Seeking either internal or external help for the national economy (e.g., for improvement of roads, new settlements, storage of food against years of bad harvest, and so on) is above suspicion. However, as an instrument in the struggle among powers, the credit system—the ingenious invention of a commercial people [England] during this century—of endlessly growing debts that remain safe against immediate demand (since the demand for payment is not made by all creditors at the same time) is a dangerous financial power. It is a war chest exceeding the treasure of all nations taken together, and it can be exhausted only by an inevitable default in taxes (although it can also be forestalled indefinitely by the economic stimulus that derives from credit's influence on industry and commerce). This ease in making war, combined with the inclination of those in power to do so—an inclination that seems innate in human nature—is a

346 great obstacle to perpetual peace. Thus, forbidding foreign debt must be a preliminary article for perpetual peace, for eventual yet unavoidable national bankruptcy must entangle many innocent nations, and that would clearly injure them. Consequently, other nations are justified in allying themselves against such a nation and its pretensions.

5. *No nation shall forcibly interfere with the constitution and government of another.*

For what can justify its doing so? Perhaps some offense that one nation's subjects give to those of another? Instead, this should serve as a warning by providing an example of the great evil that a people falls into through its lawlessness. Generally, the bad example that one free person furnishes for another (as a *scandalum acceptum*) does not injure the latter. But it would be different if, as a result of internal discord, a nation were divided in two and each part, regarding itself as a separate nation, lay claim to the whole; for (since they are in a condition of anarchy) the aid of a foreign nation to one of the parties could not be regarded as interference by the other in its constitution. So long, however, as this internal conflict remains undecided, a foreign power's interference would violate the rights of an independent people struggling with its internal ills. Doing this would be an obvious offense and would render the autonomy of every nation insecure.

6. No *nation at war with another shall permit such acts of war as shall make mutual trust impossible during some future time of peace: Such acts include the use of* Assassins (percussores) Poisoners (venefici) breach of surrender, instigation of treason (perduello) *in the opposing nation, etc.*

These are dishonorable stratagems. Some level of trust in the enemy's way of thinking must be preserved even in the midst of war, for otherwise no peace can ever be concluded and the hostilities would become a war of extermination *(bellum internecinum)*. Yet war is but a sad necessity in the sate of nature (where no tribunal empowered to make judgments supported by the power of law exists), one that maintains the rights of a nation by mere might, where neither party can be declared an unjust enemy (since this already presupposes a judgment of right) and the outcome of the conflict (as if it were a so-called "judgment of God") determines the side on which justice lies. A war of punishment *(bellum punitivum)* between nations is inconceivable (for there is no relation of superior and inferior between them). From this it follows that a war of extermination—where the destruction of both parties along with all rights is the result—would permit perpetual peace to occur only in the vast graveyard of humanity as a whole. Thus, such a war, including all means used to wage it, must be absolutely prohibited. But that the means named above inexorably lead to such war becomes clear from the following: Once they come into use, these intrinsically despicable, infernal acts cannot long be confined to war alone. This applies to the use of spies *(uti exploratoribus)*, where only the dishonorableness *of others* (which can never be entirely eliminated) is exploited; but such activities will also carry over to peacetime and will thus undermine it.

347

———

Although the laws set out above are objectively, i.e., from the perspective of the intention of those in power, merely *prohibitive laws (leges prohibitivae)*, some of them are of that *strict* kind—that is, of that class of laws that holds regardless of the circumstances *(leges strictae)*—that demands *immediate* implementaton (*viz.*, Nos. 1, 5, and 6). However, others (viz., Nos. 2, 3, 4), while not exceptions to the rule of law, do permit, depending on circumstances, some subjective leeway in their *implementation (leges latae)* as long as one does not lose sight of their end. This permission, e.g., of the *restoration* of freedom to certain nations in accord with No. 2, cannot be put off until doomsday (or as Augustus was wont to promise, *ad calendas graecas*), that is, we cannot fail to implement them. Delay is permitted only to prevent such premature implementation as might injure the intention of the article. For in the case of the second article, the prohibition concerns only the *mode of acquisition*, which is henceforth forbidden, but not the *state of ownership*, which, though not supported by the necessary title of right, was at the time (of the putative acquisition) accepted as lawful by public opinion in all nations.*

*It has previously been doubted, not unjustifiably, whether in addition to *commands (leges praeceptivae)* and *prohibitions (leges prohibitivae)* pure reason could provide *permissive laws (leges permissivae)*. For in general laws contain a foundation of objective practical necessity, while permission only provides a foundation for certain acts that depend on practical contingencies. Thus a *permissive* law would necessitate an action that one cannot be compelled to perform, which, if the object of law has the same sense in both cases, would entail a contradiction. But the permissive law here under consideration only prohibits certain modes of acquiring a right in the future (e.g., through inheritance), while the exception from this prohibition, i.e., the permission, applies to a present state of possession. In the transition from the state of nature to that of civil society, then, this possession, while unjust in itself, may nonetheless be regarded as *honest (possessio putativa)* and can continue to endure by virtue of a permissive law derived from natural right. However, as soon as any putative possession comes to be regarded as prohibited in the state of nature, every similar form of acquisition is subsequently prohibited in civil society, and this putative right to continuing possession would not hold if such a supposed acquisition had occurred in the civil state. In that case it would, as an offense against natural law, have to cease existing as soon as its illegality were discovered.

My desire here has been simply to draw the attention of proponents of natural right to the concept of a *lex permissiva*, a concept that reason in its systematically analytic use sets out and that is often used in civil (statutory) law, though with this difference, namely, that the prohibitive part of law stands on its own, while the permissive part is not (as it should be) included in the law as a limiting condition, but is regarded instead as among the exceptions to it. This means that this or that will be forbidden, *as is the case with* Nos. 1, 2, and 3, and so on indefinitely, for permissions arise only circumstantially, not according to a principle, that is, they arise only in considering specific situations. Otherwise the conditions would have to be stated in the *formulation of the prohibitive laws* and would in that way have to become laws of permission. It is therefore regrettable that the incisive, but unsolved Prize question posed by the wise and acute Count von Windischgrätz,[3] a question that directly concerns this issue, has been for-

Second Section
Which Contains the Definitive Articles for
Perpetual Peace Among Nations

The state of peace among men living in close proximity is not the
natural state *(status naturalis)*; instead, the natural state is a one of
war, which does not just consist in open hostilities, but also in the
constant and enduring threat of them.[4] The state of peace must
therefore be *established,* for the suspension of hostilities does not
provide the security of peace, and unless this security is pledged by
one neighbor to another (which can happen only in a state of *lawfulness*), the latter, from whom such security has been requested,
can treat the former as an enemy.*

---

gotten so quickly. For the possibility of a formula (such as exists in mathematics)
is the only true criterion of all subsequent legislation, and without it the so-
called *ius certum* will forever remain a pious wish. In its absence, we shall merely have *general* laws (which are valid in general), but no universal ones (which
are universally valid), and it is the latter that the concept of a law requires.

*It is commonly assumed that one ought not take hostile action against
another unless one has already been actively *injured* by that person and that is
entirely correct if both parties live in a state [governed by] *civil law.* For by
entering into civil society, each person gives every other (by virtue of the sovereignty that has power over them both) the requisite security. However, a man
(or a people) who is merely in a state of nature denies me this security and
injures me merely by being in this state. For although he does not actively
(facto) injure me, he does so by virtue of the lawlessness of his state *(statu inius-
to)*, by which he constantly threatens me, and I can require him either to enter
with me into a state of civil law or to remove himself from my surroundings.
Thus, the postulate on which all the following articles rest is: "All men who can
mutually influence one another must accept some civil constitution."
     Every just constitution, as far as the persons who accept it are concerned,
will be one of the three following:
     1. one conforming to the civil rights of men in a nation *(ius civitatis)*;
     2. one conforming to the *rights of nations* in relations to one another;
     3. one conforming to the *rights of world citizenship,* so far as men and
nations stand in mutually influential relations as citizens of a universal nation
of men *(ius cosmopoliticum)*. These are not arbitrary divisions, but ones that are
necessary in relationship to the idea of perpetual peace. Because if even only
one of these [nations] had only physical influence on another, they would be
in a state of nature, and consequently they would be bound together in a state
of war. Our intention here is to free them from this.

First Definitive Article for a Perpetual Peace
The civil constitution of every nation should be republican.

The sole established constitution that follows from the idea of an original contract, the one on which all of a nation's rightful[5] legislation must be based, is republican. For, first, it accords with the principles of the *freedom* of the members of a society (as men), second, it accords with the principles of the *dependence* of everyone on a single, common [source of] legislation (as subjects), and third, it accords with the law of equality of them all (as citizens).* Thus, so far as [the matter of] right is concerned, republicanism is the origi-

Rightful (consequently external) *freedom* cannot be defined in the way it usually is, as the privilege to do whatever one will as long as one does no injustice. For what does privilege mean? The possibility of action as long as one does no wrong. Thus, the clarification would read: Freedom is the possibility of action as long as one does no wrong. One does no wrong (one may thus do what one wills), if only one does no wrong. This is a mere empty tautology. Instead, external *(rightful) freedom* is to be clarified as follows: It is the privilege not to obey any external laws except those to which I have been able to give my consent. In just the same way, external *(rightful) equality* in a nation is that relation among citizens whereby no citizen can be bound by a law, unless all are subject to it simultaneously and in the very same way. (The principle of *rightful* dependence requires no clarification, for it is already contained in the concept of a political constitution in general.) The validity of these innate rights that necessarily and inalienably belong to humanity is confirmed and raised to an even higher level by virtue of the principle that man has rightful relations to higher beings (if he believes in them), since by these very same principles he represents himself as a citizen in the supersensuous world. Now so far as my freedom is concerned, I have no obligation even to divine laws knowable only by reason, except only insofar as I am able to consent to them. (For it is through the law of freedom that I am first able rationally to create a concept of the divine will.) But as regards the principle of equality, even the highest worldly being that I can think of (say a great Aeon)—but excepting God—has no reason (assuming I perform my duty in my position, as that Aeon performs his duty in his) to expect it to be my duty only to obey, leaving the right of command to him. This principle of *equality* does not (as does that of freedom) pertain to one's relation to God because God is the sole being excepted from the concept of duty.

Concerning all citizens' right of equality as subjects, one can resolve the issue of whether a hereditary nobility is permissible by asking whether some

nal foundation of all forms of civil constitution. Thus, the only question remaining is this, does it also provide the only foundation for perpetual peace?

Now in addition to the purity of its origin, a purity whose source   351
is the pure concept of right, the republican constitution also provides for this desirable result, namely, perpetual peace, and the reason for this is as follows: If (as must inevitably be the case, given this form of constitution) the consent of the citizenry is required in order to determine whether or not there will be war, it is natural that they consider all its calamities before committing themselves to so risky a game. (Among these are doing the fighting themselves, paying the costs of war from their own resources, having to repair at great sacrifice the war's devastation, and, finally, the ultimate evil that would make peace itself better, never being able—because of new and constant wars—to expunge the burden of debt.) By contrast, under a nonrepublican constitution, where subjects are not citizens, the easiest thing in the world to do is to declare war. Here the ruler is not a fellow citizen, but the nation's owner, and war does not affect his table, his hunt, his places of pleasure, his court festivals, and so on. Thus, he can decide to go to war for the most meaningless of reasons, as if it were a kind of pleasure party, and he can blithely leave its justification (which decency requires) to his diplomatic corps, who are always prepared for such exercises.

----

rank making one citizen superior to another granted by the nation is antecedent to *merit*, or whether merit must precede rank. Now clearly, when rank is tied to birth it is completely uncertain whether merit (skill and integrity in one's office) will accompany it. Consequently, this hereditary arrangement is no different from conferring command on some favorite person who is wholly lacking in merit. This is something that the general will of a people would never agree to in an original contract (which is the principle that underlies all rights). For a nobleman is not, by virtue of that fact alone, a *noble* man. Concerning the *nobility of office* (as one can designate the rank of a higher magistrate, which one must earn by virtue of merit), here rank does not belong to the person, but to the position he holds, and this does not violate [the principle of] equality, because when that person resigns his office he gives up his rank at the same time and again becomes one of the people.

352   The following comments are necessary to prevent confusing (as so often happens) the republican form of constitution with the democratic one: The forms of a nation *(civitas)* can be analyzed either on the basis of the persons who possess the highest political authority or on the basis of the way the people are *governed* by their ruler, whoever he may be. The first is called the form of sovereignty *(forma imperii)*, of which only three kinds are possible, specifically, where either *one*, or *several* in association, or *all* those together who make up civil society possess the sovereign power (autocracy, aristocracy, and democracy, the power of a monarch, the power of a nobility, the power of a people). The second is the form of government *(forma regiminis)* and concerns the way in which a nation, based on its constitution (the act of the general will whereby a group becomes a people), exercises its authority. In this regard, government is either *republican* or *despotic. Republicanism* is that political principle whereby executive power (the government) is separated from legislative power. In a despotism the ruler independently executes laws that it has itself made; here rulers have taken hold of the public will and treated it as their own private will. Among the three forms of government, *democracy*, in the proper sense of the term, is necessarily a *despotism*, because it sets up an executive power in which all citizens make decisions about and, if need be, against one (who therefore does not agree); consequently, all, who are not quite all, decide, so that the general will contradicts both itself and freedom.

Every form of government that is not *representative* is properly speaking *without form*, because one and the same person can no more be at one and the same time the legislator and executor of his will (than the universal proposition can serve as the major premise in a syllogism and at the same time be the subsumption of the particular under it in the minor premise). And although the other two forms of political constitution are defective inasmuch as they always leave room for a democratic form of government, it is nonetheless possible that they assume a form of government that accords with the *spirit* of a representative system: As Friederick II[6] at least *said*, "I
353   am merely the nation's highest servant."* The democratic system

---

*People have often criticized the lofty titles that are normally bestowed on a ruler ("the divinely anointed" and "the representative and executor of the divine will on earth") as gross and extravagant flatteries; but it seems to me that this is without basis. Far from stirring arrogance in the ruler of a country, they

makes this impossible, for everyone wants to rule. One can therefore say, the smaller the number of persons who exercise the power of the nation (the number of rulers), the more they represent and the closer the political constitution approximates the possibility of republicanism, and thus, the constitution can hope through gradual reforms finally to become republican. For this reason, attaining this state that embodies a completely just constitution is more difficult in an aristocracy than in a monarchy, and, except by violent revolution, there is no possibility of attaining it in a democracy. Nonetheless, the people are incomparably more concerned with the form of government* than with the form of the constitution (although a great deal depends on the degree to which the latter is suited to the goals of the former). But if the form of government is to cohere with the concept of right, it must include the representative system, which is possible only in a republican form of government and without which (no matter what the constitution may be) government is despotic and brutish. None of the ancient so-called republics were aware of this, and consequently they inevitably degenerated into despotism; still, this is more bearable under a single person's rulership than other forms of government are.

---

should instead humble his soul, providing he possesses reason (which one must assume) and has reflected on the fact that he has undertaken an office that is too great for a single man, the holiest one that God has established on earth, the protector of the *rights of mankind*, and he must always be careful not to tread upon this apple of God's eye.

*In his important sounding but hollow and empty language, Mallet du Pan[7] boasts of having after many years of experience finally come to be convinced of Pope's well known saying, "For forms of government let fools contest;/Whate're is best administered is best."[8] If that means that the best administered government is the best administered, then he has, in Swift's expression, "cracked a nut and been rewarded with only a worm." But if it means that it is the best form of government, i.e., political constitution, then it is fundamentally false, for good governments prove nothing about form of government. Who has ruled better than a Titus and a Marcus Aurelius, and yet one was succeeded by a Domitian and the other by Commodus, which could not have happened under a good political constitution, since their unfitness for the post was known early enough and the power of the ruler was sufficient to have excluded them from it.

Second Definitive Article for a Perpetual Peace
The right of nations shall be based on a federation of free states.

As nations, peoples can be regarded as single individuals who injure one another through their close proximity while living in the state of nature (i.e., independently of external laws). For the sake of its own security, each nation can and should demand that the others enter into a contract resembling the civil one and guaranteeing the rights of each. This would be a federation of *nations*, but it must not be a nation consisting of nations. The latter would be contradictory, for in every nation there exists the relation of *ruler* (legislator) to *subject* (those who obey, the people); however, many nations in a single nation would constitute only a single nation, which contradicts our assumption (since we are here weighing the rights of *nations* in relation to one another, rather than fusing them into a single nation).

Just as we view with deep disdain the attachment of savages to their lawless freedom—preferring to scuffle without end rather than to place themselves under lawful restraints that they themselves constitute, consequently preferring a mad freedom to a rational one—and consider it barbarous, rude, and brutishly degrading of humanity, so also should we think that civilized peoples (each one united into a nation) would hasten as quickly as possible to escape so similar a state of abandonment. Instead, however, each *nation* sees its majesty (for it is absurd to speak of the majesty of a people) to consist in not being subject to any external legal constraint, and the glory of its ruler consists in being able, without endangering himself, to command many thousands to sacrifice themselves for a matter that does not concern them.* The primary difference between Euro-pean and American savages is this, while many latter tribes have been completely eaten by their enemies, the former know how to make better use of those they have conquered than to consume them: They increase the number of their subjects and thus also the quantity of instruments they have to wage even more extensive wars.

---

*Thus a Bulgarian prince gave this answer to a Greek emperor who kindly offered to settle a conflict between them by duel: "A smith who has tongs will not use his hands to take the glowing iron from the fire."

Given the depravity of human nature which is revealed and can be glimpsed in the free relations among nations (though deeply concealed by governmental restraints in law governed civil-society), one must wonder why the word *right* has not been completely discarded from the politics of war as pedantic, or why no nation has openly ventured to declare that it should be. For while, Hugo Grotius, Pufendorf, Vattel,[9] and others whose philosophically and diplomatically formulated codes do not and cannot have the slightest legal force (since nations do not stand under any common external constraints), are always piously cited in justification of a war of aggression (and who therefore provide only cold comfort), no example can be given of a nation having foregone its intention [of going to war] based on the arguments provided by such important men. The homage that every nation pays (at least in words) to the concept of right proves, nonetheless, that there is in man a still greater, though presently dormant, moral aptitude to master the evil principle in himself (a principle he cannot deny) and to hope that others will also overcome it. For otherwise the word *right* would never leave the mouths of those nations that want to make war on one another, unless it were mockingly, as when that Gallic prince declared, "Nature has given the strong the prerogative of making the weak obey them."

Nations can press for their rights only by waging war and never in a trial before an independent tribunal, but war and its favorable consequence, victory, cannot determine the right. And although a *treaty of peace* can put an end to some particular war, it cannot end the state of war (the tendency always to find a new pretext for war). (And this situation cannot straightforwardly be declared unjust, since in this circumstance each nation is judge of its own case.) Nor can one say of nations as regards their rights what one can say concerning the natural rights of men in a state of lawlessness, to wit, that "they should abandon this state." (For as nations they already have an internal, legal constitution and therefore have outgrown the compulsion to subject themselves to another legal constitution that is subject to someone else's concept of right.) Nonetheless, from the throne of its moral legislative power, reason absolutely condemns war as a means of determining the right and makes seeking the state of peace a matter of unmitigated duty. But without a contract among nations peace can be neither inaugurated nor guaranteed. A league of a special sort must therefore be established, one that we can call a *league of peace (foedus pacifi-cum)*, which will be distinguished from a *treaty of peace (pactum pacis)* because the latter seeks merely to stop one war, while the former seeks to end *all* wars forever. This league does not seek any power of the sort possessed by nations, but only the maintenance and security of each nation's own freedom, as well as that of the other nations leagued with it, without their having thereby to subject themselves to civil laws and their constraints (as men in the state of nature must do). It can be shown that this *idea of federalism* should eventually include all nations and thus lead to perpetual peace. For if good fortune should so dispose matters that a powerful and enlightened people should form a republic (which by its nature must be inclined to seek perpetual peace), it will provide a focal point for a federation association among other nations that will join it in order to guarantee a state of peace among nations that is in accord with the idea of the right of nations, and through several associations of this sort such a federation can extend further and further.

That a people might say, "There should be no war among us, for we want to form ourselves into a nation, i.e., place ourselves under a supreme legislative, executive, and judicial power to resolve our conflicts peacefully," is understandable. But when a nation says, "There should be no war between me and other nations, though I recognize no supreme legislative power to guarantee me my rights and him his," then if there does not exist a surrogate of the union in a civil society, which is a free federation, it is impossible to understand what the basis for so entrusting my rights is. Such a federation is necessarily tied rationally to the concept of the right of nations, at least if this latter notion has any meaning.

The concept of the right of nations as a right to go to war is meaningless (for it would then be the right to determine the right not by independent, universally valid laws that restrict the freedom of everyone, but by one-sided maxims backed by force). Consequently, the concept of the right of nations must be understood as follows: that it serves justly those men who are disposed to seek one another's destruction and thus find perpetual peace in the grave that covers all the horrors of violence and its perpetrators. Reason can provide related nations with no other means for emerging from the state of lawlessness, which consists solely of war, than that they give up their savage (lawless) freedom, just as individual persons do, and, by accommodating themselves to the constraints of common law, establish a *nation of peoples (civitas gentium),* that (continuingly growing) will finally include all the people of the earth. But they do not will to do this because it does not conform to their idea of the right of nations, and consequently they discard in *hypothesis* what is true in *thesis.* So (if everything is not to be lost) in place of the positive idea of *a world republic* they put only the *negative* surrogate of an enduring, ever expanding *federation* that prevents war and curbs the tendency of that hostile inclination to defy the law, though there will always be constant danger of their breaking loose. (*Furor impius intus—fremit horridus ore cruento.* Vergil).*10

Third Definitive Article for a Perpetual Peace **Cosmopolitan right** *shall be limited to conditions of universal* hospitality.

As in the preceding articles, our concern here is not with philanthropy but with *right,* and in this context *hospitality* (hospitableness) means the right of an alien not to be treated as an enemy upon his arrival in another's country. If it can be done without destroying him, he can be turned away; but, as long as he behaves peaceably he cannot be treated as an enemy. He may request the *right* to be a *permanent visitor* (which would require a special, charitable agree- 358

*It would not be inappropriate at the end of a war concluded by peace for a people to set aside, after a festival of thanksgiving, a day of atonement so that in the name of the nation they might ask heaven to forgive them for the great sin that the human race continues to be guilty of by failing to establish a lawful contract in relation to other peoples, preferring instead, through pride in their independence, to employ the barbarous means of war (by use of which they cannot secure what they seek, namely, the rights of each particular nation). The festivals of thanksgiving for victories during war, the hymns that are sung (in good Israelitic fashion) to the *Lord of Lords,* could not stand in greater contrast with the ideas of a Father of men, for besides displaying an indifference to the way in which peoples seek their mutual right (which is sad enough), they actually express joy at having destroyed numerous humans and their happiness.

ment to make him a fellow inhabitant for a certain period), but the *right to visit*, to associate, belongs to all men by virtue of their common ownership of the earth's surface; for since the earth is a globe, they cannot scatter themselves infinitely, but must, finally, tolerate living in close proximity, because originally no one had a greater right to any region of the earth than anyone else. Uninhabitable parts of this surface—the sea and deserts—separate these communities, and yet ships and camels (the *ships* of the desert) make it possible to approach one another across these unowned regions, and the right to the *earth's surface* that belongs in common to the totality of men makes commerce possible. The inhospitableness that coastal dwellers (e.g., on the Barbary Coast) show by robbing ships in neighboring seas and by making slaves of stranded seafarers, or of desert dwellers (the Arabic Bedouins), who regard their proximity to nomadic peoples as giving them a right to plunder, is contrary to natural right, even though the latter extends the right to hospitality, i.e., the privilege of aliens to enter, only so far as makes attempts at commerce with native inhabitants possible. In this way distant parts of the world can establish with one another peaceable relations that will eventually become matters of public law, and the human race can gradually be brought closer and closer to a cosmopolitan constitution.

Compare this with the inhospitable conduct of civilized nations in our part of the world, especially commercial ones: The injustice that they display towards foreign lands and peoples (which is the same as *conquering* them), is terrifying. When discovered, America, the lands occupied by the blacks, the Spice Islands, the Cape, etc., were regarded as lands belonging to no one because their inhabitants were counted for nothing. Foreign soldiers were imported into East India under the pretext of merely establishing economic relations, and with them came subjection of the natives, incitement of various nations to widespread wars among themselves, famine, rebellion, treachery, and the entire litany of evils that can afflict the human race.

China* and Japan (*Nippon*), which have had experience with

359

*[For the reasons why] we should call this great kingdom by the name it gives itself (namely, China, not Sina, or anything similar), one has only to consult Georgi's *Alpha [betum] Tibet [anum}*, pp. 651–4, especially note b. According to the observation of Professor Fischer of Petersburg, there is actu-

such guests, have therefore wisely restricted contact with them. China only permits contact with a single European people, the Dutch, whom they nonetheless exclude as if they were prisoners from associating with the natives. The worst (or, considered from the perspective of a moral judge, the best) consequence of all this is that such violence profits these trading companies not at all and that all of them are at the point of near collapse. The Sugar Islands, the

---

ally no determinate name that it uses in reference to itself. The most common one is the word *"Kin,"* namely, gold (which the Tibetans call *"Ser"*), and therefore the emperor is called the king of *Gold* (i.e., of the most magnificent country in the world). In the kingdom itself, this word is probably pronounced *"Chen,"* but is pronounced *"Kin"* by the Italian missionaries (who cannot make the guttural sound). From this one can see that the Roman's so-called "Land of Seres" was China, and silk was brought from there to Europe across *Greater-Tibet* (probably through *Lesser Tibet,* Bukhara, Persia and so on). This leads to many speculations concerning the antiquity of this amazing nation in comparison with that of Hindustan, as well as regarding its connections with Tibet and also with Japan. But the name Sina or Tshina, which neighbors of this land give it, leads nowhere. Perhaps this also allows us to clarify the very ancient but never properly understood commerce of Europe with Tibet from what *Hysichius* has recorded about the hierophant's cry "Κονε Ομπαξ" *(Konx Ompax)* in the Eleusinian mysteries. (See *Travels of the Young Anacharsis*, Part V, p. 447f.) For according to Georgi's *Alph. Tibet.*, the word *"Concoia"* means God, which has a striking resemblance to Knox. *Pah-cio* (*ibid.*, p. 520), which the Greeks might well have pronounced *pax*, means the *promulgator legis*, the divinity that pervades all of nature (also called *Cencresi*, p. 177). However, *Om*, which La Croze translated *benedictus, blessed*, can be related to divinity, but probably means nothing other than the *beatified*, p. 507. Now Fr. Franz Horatius often asked the Tibetan Lamas what they understood God *(Concioa)* to be and always received this answer, "It is the gathering of all the Saints" (i.e., the gathering of all blessed ones who, according to the Lama's doctrine of rebirth, have finally returned, after many migrations through all sorts of bodies, to the divinity, or *Burchane*, i.e., souls metamorphosed into being that is worthy of worship, p. 233). Thus that mysterious term *Konx Ompax* might well refer to that *holy (Konx)*, *blessed (Om)* and *wise (Pax)* supreme Being who pervades the world (nature personified), and its use in the Greek *Mystery religions* may have signified a monotheism to the Epopts that contrasted with the polytheism of the people, though Fr. Horatius (among others) detected an *atheism* in it. But just how that mysterious term made its way from Tibet to Greece may apparently be explained in the foregoing way, as well as Europe's early commerce with China (which may have begun earlier than with Hindustan) through Tibet.

seat of the cruellest and most ingenious slavery, yield no true profit, but serve only the indirect and not very profitable purpose of training sailors for ships of war, which in turn aids the pursuit of wars in Europe. And this is the action of powers who, while imbibing injustice like water, make much of their piety and who in matters of orthodoxy want to be regarded as the elect.

360   Because a (narrower or wider) community widely prevails among the Earth's peoples, a transgression of rights in *one* place in the world is felt *everywhere*; consequently, the idea of cosmopolitan right is not fantastic and exaggerated, but rather an amendment to the unwritten code of national and international rights, necessary to the public rights of men in general. Only such amendment allows us to flatter ourselves with the thought that we are making continual progress towards perpetual peace.

First Supplement
on the Guarantee of Perpetual Peace

Perpetual peace is *insured* (guaranteed) by nothing less than that great artist *nature (natura daedala rerum)*[11] whose mechanical process makes her purposiveness[12] visibly manifest, permitting harmony to emerge among men through their discord, even against their wills. If we regard this design as a compulsion resulting from

361   one of her causes whose laws of operation are unknown to us, we call it *fate*, while, if we reflect on nature's purposiveness in the flow of world events, and regard it to be the underlying wisdom of a higher cause that directs the human race toward its objective goal and

362   predetermines the world's course, we call it *providence.** We cannot actually have *cognitive* knowledge of these intricate designs in

---

*There is manifest in the mechanism of nature to which man (as a sensory being) belongs a form that is fundamental to its existence, a form that we cannot conceive except insofar as it underlies the purpose of a predetermining creator of the world. We call this predetermination (divine) *providence* in general; so far as it is established at the *beginning* of the world, we call it *grounding providence (providentia conditrix; semel iussit, semper parent*, Augustine);[13] where this purposiveness in nature's course is maintained through universal laws, we call it *ruling providence (providentia gubernatrix)*; where it leads to specific ends that men cannot foresee but can only infer from its results, we call it *guiding*

nature, nor can we *infer* their actual existence from it, but (as with all relations between the forms of things and purposes in general) we can and must *attribute* them to objects only in thought so as to conceive of their possibility on an analogy with mankind's productive activities. The relationship of objects to and their conformity

---

providence (providentia directrix); finally, where we regard particular events as divine ends, we no longer speak of providence but of *dispensation (directio extraordinaria)*. However, it is a foolish presumption for men to want to be able to recognize these latter for what they are (for in fact they are miracles, even though the events are not described in that way). No matter how pious and humble such language may be, it is absurd and altogether self-conceited to make an inference from some single event to some special principle as its efficient cause (so that this event is [regarded as] an end and not merely the natural and mechanical consequence of some other end completely unknown to us). In the same way, applying the distinction between *universal* and *special* providence (considered *materially*) to *objects* in the world is unjustifiable and self-contradictory (as when, for example, one claims that nature is concerned to preserve the species, but leaves individuals to chance); for the point of saying that providence applies universally is that no single thing is taken into consideration. Presumably, one intends by this to distinguish between the ways in which providence (considered *formally*) carries out its intentions, that is, in ordinary [fashion] (e.g., the annual death and revival of nature in accordance with the change of seasons) or in *extraordinary* fashion (e.g., the transport of wood by ocean currents to icebound coasts, where it cannot grow, so as to provide for the needs of their natives, who could not live without it). Here, while we can readily explain the physical and mechanical causes of these appearances to ourselves (e.g., by the fact that the banks of rivers in temperate lands are heavily wooded so that trees fall into them and are carried off by the Gulf Stream), we must nonetheless not overlook teleological causes, which indicate the care of a wisdom that governs nature. Only the scholastic concept of a divine *participation* in or concurrence *(concursus)* with every effect experienced in the world of sense must be given up. *First,* that scholastic view attempts to conjoin dissimilar kinds of things *(gryphes iungere equis)*[14] and it is self-contradictory to let that which is itself the wholly sufficient cause of all changes in the world supplement its own predetermining providence in the course of the world (implying that providence must originally have therefore been lacking). It is, for example, self-contradictory to say that *after God,* the physician assisted in curing the illness. For *causa solitaria non iuvat.*[15] God creates the physician and all his medicines, and if we want to go back to the highest, but theoretically inconceivable,[16] original cause we must ascribe the action entirely to Him. Of course, if we explain this event as following from the chain of causes in the world and in accordance with the natural order, one can ascribe healing to the physician alone. *Second,* with that scholastic way of

with the purposes that reason itself sets out for us (the end of moral-ity) can be represented from a *theoretical* point of view as a tran-scendent idea, but from the practical point of view (where, e.g., it is employed in relation to our concept of duty regarding *perpetual peace*), it is represented as a dogmatic idea and it is here that its real-ity is properly established. When, as in the context of this essay, our concern is entirely theoretical (and not religious) it is most appro-priate to the limits of human reason to use the term *nature* (for in reflecting on the relations of effects to their causes, human reason must remain within the bounds of possible experience); the term *nature* is less *pretentious* than a term connoting that there is a *prov-idence* of which we can have cognitive knowledge, and on which we take flight as on Icarus's wings in order more closely to approach the secrets of some unfathomable intention.

Before we define this guarantee [of perpetual peace] more close-ly, we must examine the state in which nature has placed her actors on her vast stage, a state that ultimately and necessarily secures their peace—then we shall see how she guarantees the latter.

363

Nature's provisional arrangement consists of the following: 1. She has taken care that men can live in all regions of the world. 2. Through *war* she has driven them everywhere, even into the most inhospitable regions in order to populate them. 3. Also through war she has constrained them to establish more or less legal relation-ships. It is truly wonderful that moss grows even in the cold wastes by the Arctic Ocean and that *reindeer* can dig it from beneath the snow so that they can become food or transportation for the Ostiak or Samoyed; or that the salt deserts are inhabited by the *camel*, which appears to have been created for traveling over them, so that the deserts do not go unused. But purpose is even more clearly evi-dent when one realizes that not only do furbearing animals exist on

---

thinking we give up all determinant principles for making judgments about an effect. But from a *morally-practical* perspective (which is wholly directed to the supersensuous)—e.g., in the belief that if only our interactions are pure, God will compensate for our own injustices by means that are inconceivable to us and that we should not, therefore, give up our striving to do good—the concept of a divine *concursus* is entirely appropriate and even necessary. But it is self-evident that one must not attempt to *explain* a good action (as an event in the world) in this way, for that is a vain and consequently absurd attempt at theo-retical knowledge of the supersensuous.

the shores of the Arctic Ocean, but also seals, walruses, and whales, whose flesh provides food and whose blubber provides warmth for the inhabitants. However, what most arouses our wonder is nature's care to bring (in what way we do not really know) driftwood to these barren regions, for without this material the natives could have neither their canoes and spears nor their huts to dwell in. In these regions they are sufficiently occupied with their war against animals that they live in peace among themselves. But it was probably nothing but war that *drove* them there. Among all the animals, the *horse* was the first that man learned to tame and to domesticate in the process of populating the earth and the first *instrument of war* (for the elephant belongs to a later period, to the luxury of already established nations). The art of cultivating certain kinds of grasses, called *grains*, whose original characteristics are no longer known, as well as the propagation and refinement of various *fruits* by transplanting and grafting (in Europe perhaps only two species, the crab apple and the wild pear), could arise only under conditions provided by already established nations, where property was secure; and it could occur only after men had already undergone the transition from the lawless freedom of hunting,* fishing, and herding to the life of *agriculture*. *Salt* and *iron* were discovered next, and these were proba-   364
bly the first articles of trade sought far and wide by different peoples. In this way they entered into *peaceful relations* with one another, and from this common understanding, community of interest and peaceful relations arose with the most distant peoples.

In taking care that men *could* live everywhere on earth, nature has also despotically chosen that they *should* live everywhere, even against their inclinations, and without presupposing that this should rest on a concept of duty that binds men as a moral law; instead, she

---

*Of all forms of life, the *life of the hunter* is without doubt most contrary to a civilized constitution, for, having to live separately, families soon become estranged and, dispersed as they become in immense forest, also soon become enemies, for each requires a great deal of room in order to provide for its nourishment and clothing. The Noachic prohibition against blood (Gen. 9:4–5) (is repeated often, and Jewish Christians imposed it on pagans newly converted to Christianity as a condition of their acceptance, though for different reasons, Acts 15:20, 21:25) appears originally to have been nothing other than a command against the *hunting life*, since the latter often required eating raw flesh, and when the later is forbidden, the other must also be.

has chosen war as the means whereby this purpose is to be fulfilled. Specifically, we see peoples whose unity of language reveals the unity of their origins, for instance, the *Samoyeds* of the Arctic Ocean, on the one hand, and a people with a similar language living two hundred miles distant, in the Altai Mountains, on the other; between them lives another people, of Mongolian origin, who are adept at horsemanship and, consequently, war and who drove the two parts of the other race into inhospitable arctic regions, where they would certainly not have gone of their own inclination.* Similarly, in the northern-most regions of Europe, Gothic and Sarmitic peoples, who pushed their way in, separated the *Finns*, called *Lapps*, by an equal distance from the linguistically related *Hungarians*. And what else but war—which nature uses as a means to populate the entire earth—could have driven the Eskimos (who are perhaps very ancient European adventurers, and totally distinct as a race from all Americans) to the north, and the Pescherais to the south of America, to Tierra del Fuego. Nonetheless, war itself requires no particular motivation, but appears to be ingrained in human nature and is even valued as something noble; indeed, the desire for glory inspires men to it, even independently of selfish motives. Consequently, *courage in war* (among American Indians as well as during Europe's chivalric period) is judged to be of immediate and great worth not only *during war* (as is reasonable), but also in order that *war might be*, and often war is begun only as a means to display courage. As a result, an intrinsic worth is bestowed on war, even to the extent that philosophers, unmindful of that Greek saying, "War is a bad bet because it produces more evil people than it eliminates," have praised it as having a certain ennobling influence on mankind. So much for what nature does to further *her own ends* in respect to the human race as a class of animal.

---

*One could ask, if nature has chosen that these icy coasts should not remain uninhabited and if (as we can expect) nature no longer provides them with driftwood, what will become of their inhabitants? For one must believe that as culture progresses, the natives in the temperate zone might make better use of the wood that grows on the banks of their rivers if they did not allow it to fall into rivers and float away into the sea. I answer: Those who dwell along the Ob, the Yenisei, the Lena, etc., will provide it through trade, exchanging it for products from the animal kingdom, in which the sea along the Arctic coasts abounds—but only if she (nature) first compels them to peace.

Our concern now is the most important question regarding the objective of perpetual peace: How does nature further this purpose that man's own reason sets out as a duty for him, i.e., how does she foster his *moral objective*, and how has it been guaranteed that what man ought to do through the laws of freedom, but does not, he shall, notwithstanding his freedom, do through nature's constraint? This question arises with respect to all three aspects of public right, *civil, international, and cosmopolitan right*. When I say of nature that she *wills* that this or that happen, that does not mean that she sets it out as a duty that we do it (because only practical reason, which is free of constraint, can do that); rather, she does it herself whether or not we will it *(fata volentem ducunt, nolentem trahunt)*.[17]

1. Even if a people were not constrained by internal discord to submit to public laws, war would make them do it, for according to the natural arrangement explained above, every people finds itself neighbor to another people that threatens it, and it must form itself into a *nation* so as to be able to prepare itself to meet this threat with *military might*. Now the republican constitution is the only one wholly compatible with the rights of men, but it is also the most difficult to establish and still harder to maintain, so much so that many contend that a republic must be a nation of *angels*, for men's self-seeking inclinations make them incapable of adhering to so sublime a form of government. But now nature comes to the aid of that revered but practically impotent general will, which is grounded in reason. Indeed, this aid comes directly from those self-seeking inclinations, and it is merely by organizing the nation well (which is certainly within man's capacities) that they are able to direct their power against one another, and one inclination is able to check or cancel the destructive tendencies of the others. The result for reason is the same as if neither sets of opposing inclinations existed, and so man, even though he is not morally good, is forced to be a good citizen. As hard as it may sound, the problem of organizing a nation is solvable even for a people comprised of devils (if only they possess understanding). The problem can be stated in this way: "So order and organize a group of rational beings who require universal laws for their preservation—though each is secretly inclined to exempt himself from such laws—that, while their private attitudes conflict, these nonetheless so cancel one another that these beings behave publicly just as if they had no evil attitudes." This kind of problem must be *solvable*. For it does not require the moral improvement of man; it requires only that we know how to apply the mechanism of

366

nature to men so as to organize the conflict of hostile attitudes present in a people in such a way that they must compel one another to submit to coercive laws and thus to enter into a state of peace, where laws have power. One can see that although the inner core of morality is certainly not its cause, presently existing but still very imperfectly organized nations have in their foreign relations already approached what the idea of right prescribes (so that a good national constitution cannot be expected to arise from morality, but, rather, quite the opposite, a people's good moral condition is to be expected only under a good constitution). Consequently, the mechanism of nature, in which self-seeking inclinations naturally counteract one another in their external relations, can be used by reason as a means to prepare the way for its own end, the rule of right, as well as to promote and secure the nation's internal and external peace. This means that nature irresistibly *wills* that right should finally triumph. What one neglects to do will ultimately occur of its own accord, though with a great deal of inconvenience. "If one bends the reed too much, it breaks; and whoever wills too much, wills nothing."[18]

2. The idea of international right presupposes the existence of many *separate*, independent, adjoining nations; and although such a situation is in itself a state of war (assuming that a federative union among them does not prevent the outbreak of hostilities), yet this situation is rationally preferable to their being overrun by a superior power that melds them into a universal monarchy. For laws invariably lose their impact with the expansion of their domain of governance, and after it has uprooted the soul of good a soulless despotism finally degenerates into anarchy. Nonetheless, the desire of every nation (or its ruler) is to establish an enduring peace, hoping, if possible, to dominate the entire world. But nature *wills* otherwise. She uses two means to prevent peoples from intermingling and to separate them, differences in *language* and *religion*,* which do

---

Differences in religion: an odd expression! Just as if one spoke of different *moralities*. No doubt there can be different kinds of historical *faiths*, though these do not pertain to religion, but only to the history of the means used to promote it, and these are the province of learned investigation; the same holds of different religious *books* (*Zendavesta*, the *Vedas*, *Koran*, and so on). But there is only a single *religion*, valid for all men in all times. Those [faiths and books] can thus be nothing more than the accidental vehicles of religion and can only thereby be different in different times and places.

367

indeed dispose men to mutual hatred and to pretexts for war. But the growth of culture and men's gradual progress toward greater agreement regarding their principles lead to mutual understanding and peace. Unlike that peace that despotism (in the graveyard of freedom) brings about by vitiating all powers, this one is produced and secured by an equilibrium of the liveliest competing powers.

3. Just as nature wisely separates peoples that the will of every nation, based on principles of international right, would gladly unite through cunning or force, so also by virtue of their mutual interest does nature unite peoples against violence and war, for the concept of cosmopolitan right does not protect them from it. The *spirit of trade* cannot coexist with war, and sooner or later this spirit dominates every people. For among all those powers (or means) that belong to a nation, financial power may be the most reliable in forcing nations to pursue the noble cause of peace (though not from moral motives); and wherever in the world war threatens to break out, they will try to head it off through mediation, just as if they were permanently leagued for this purpose. By the very nature of things, large alliances for [purposes of waging] war are very rare and are even more rarely successful. In this fashion nature guarantees perpetual peace by virtue of the mechanism of man's inclinations themselves; to be sure, it does not do so with a certainty sufficient to *prophesy* it from a theoretical point of view, but we can do so from a practical one, which makes it our duty to work toward bringing about this goal (which is not a chimerical one).

Second Supplement
Secret Article for Perpetual Peace

Objectively, i.e., in the terms of its content, a secret article in proceedings concerning public right is a contradiction; but subjectively, i.e., judged from the perspective of the kind of person who dictates it, an article can certainly contain a secret [provision], for a person may find it beneath his dignity to declare openly that he is its author.

The sole article of this kind is contained in this sentence: *The maxims of philosophers concerning the conditions under which public peace is possible shall be consulted by nations armed for war.*

While it seems humiliating for the legislative authority of a nation, to whom we must naturally ascribe the greatest wisdom, to seek instruction from *subjects* (the philosophers) concerning the principles on which it should act toward other nations, yet it is very advisable to do so. Thus, the nation will *silently* (that is secretly) *seek their advice,* which is to say, it will *allow* them *to speak* freely and publicly about the universal maxims concerning the conduct of war and the search for peace (for they do it of their own accord already, if only one does not forbid it). And an arrangement concerning this issue among nations does not require a special agreement, since it is already present as an obligation in universal (morally legislative) human reason. This does not, however, mean that the nation must give the principles of the philosophers precedence over the decisions of the jurist (the representatives of national power), but only that they be *heard.* The jurist, who has adopted as his symbol not only the *scales* of right but also the *sword* of justice, normally uses the latter not merely to keep the alien influences away from the former, but when one side of the scales will not sink, to throw the sword into it *(vae victis).*[19] Every jurist who is not at the same time a philosopher (even in morality), is severely tempted by this practice; but his only function is to apply existing laws and to investigate whether they require improvement, even though, because his function is invested with power (as are the other two), he regards it as the higher one, when, in fact, it is the lower. The philosophical faculty[20] occupies a very low position in the face of the combined power of the other two. Thus it is said, for example, that philosophy is the *handmaid* of theology (and this is said of the two others as well). But one does not rightly know "whether this handmaid carries the torch before her gracious lady or bears her train behind her."

That kings should be philosophers, or philosophers kings is neither to be expected nor to be desired, for the possession of power inevitably corrupts reason's free judgment. However, that kings or sovereign peoples (who rule themselves by laws of equality) should not allow the class of philosophers to disappear or to be silent, but should permit them to speak publicly is indispensable to the enlightenment of their affairs. And because this class is by nature incapable of sedition and of forming cliques, it cannot be suspected of being the formulator of *propaganda.*

369

Appendix

I
On the Disagreement between Morals and Politics in
Relation to Perpetual Peace

Taken objectively, morality is in itself practical, for it is the totality of unconditionally binding laws according to which we *ought* to act, and once one has acknowledged the authority of its concept of duty, it would be utterly absurd to continue wanting to say that one *cannot* do his duty. For if that were so, then this concept would disappear from morality *(ultra posse nemo obligatur)*;[21] consequently, there can be no conflict between politics as an applied doctrine of right and morals as a theoretical doctrine of right (thus no conflict between practice and theory). [If such a conflict were to occur], one would have to understand morality as a universal *doctrine of prudence*, i.e., a theory of maxims by which to choose the most efficient means of furthering one's own interests, which is to deny that morality exists at all.

Politics says, *"Be ye wise as serpents,"* to which morality adds (as a limiting condition), "and innocent as doves."[22] Where both of these maxims cannot coexist in a command, there one finds an actual conflict between politics and morality; but if the two are completely united the concept of opposition is absurd, and the question as to how the conflict is to be resolved cannot even be posed as a problem. However, the proposition, *"Honesty is the best policy,"* is beyond all refutation, and is the indispensable condition of all policy. The divinity who protects the boundaries of morality does not yield to Jupiter (the protector of power), for the latter is still subject to fate. That is, reason is not yet sufficiently enlightened that it can survey the series of predetermining causes and predict with certainty what the happy or unhappy consequences that follow in accord with nature's mechanism from men's activities will be (though one can hope that they come out as one wishes). But with respect to everything we have to do in order to remain on the path of duty (according to rules of wisdom), reason does provide us with enlightenment sufficient to pursue our ultimate goals.

Now even if the practical man (for whom morality is mere theo-
ry) admits that we can do what we ought to do, he bases his disconsolate rejection of our fond hope on the following consideration: He asserts that, human nature being what it is, we can predict that man will never want to do what is required to achieve the goal of perpet-

ual peace. Certainly, the will of all *individual* men (the *distributive* unity of the wills of *all*) to live under a lawful constitution that accords with principles of freedom is not sufficient to attain this goal; only the will of *all together* (the *collective* unity of combined wills) is. The solution to so difficult a task requires that civil society become a whole. Implementing this state of right (in practice) can begin only with *force*, and this coercion will subsequently provide a basis for public right, because an additional unifying cause must be superimposed on the differences among each person's particular desires in order to transform them into a common will—and this is something no single person can do. Furthermore, in actual experience we can certainly anticipate great deviations from that (theoretical) idea of right (for we can hardly expect the legislator to have such moral sensibilities that having united the wild mass into a people, he will then allow them to create a legal constitution through their general will).

For this reason it is said that he who once has power in hand will not have laws prescribed to him by the people. And once a nation is no longer subject to external laws it will not allow itself to be subjected to the judgment of other nations regarding the way in which it should seek to uphold its rights against them. Even a continent that feels itself to be superior to another, regardless of whether or not the latter stands in the way of the former, will not fail to exercise the means of increasing its power, plundering and conquering. Thus, all theoretical plans for civil, international, and cosmopolitan rights dissolve into empty, impractical ideals; by contrast, a practice that is based on empirical principles of human nature and that does not regard it demeaning to formulate its maxims in accord with the way of the world can alone hope to find a secure foundation for its structure of political prudence.

372   To be sure, if neither freedom nor the moral law that is based on it exist, and if everything that happens or can happen is mere mechanism of nature, then politics (as the art of using that mechanism to govern men) would be the whole of practical wisdom, and the concept of right would be contentless thought. But if we find it absolutely necessary to couple politics with the concept of right, and even to make the latter a limiting condition of politics, the compatibility of the two must be conceded. I can actually think of a *moral politician*, i.e., one who so interprets the principles of political prudence that they can be coherent with morality, but I cannot think of a *political moralist*, i.e., one who forges a morality to suit the statesman's advantage.

The moral politician will make it a principle that once a fault that could not have been anticipated is found in a nation's constitution or in its relations with other nations, it becomes a duty, particularly for the rulers of nations, to consider how it can be corrected as soon as possible and in such a way as to conform with natural right, which stands in our eyes as a model presented by an idea of reason; and this ought to be done even at the cost of self-sacrifice. Since it is contrary to all political prudence consistent with morality to sever a bond of political or cosmopolitan union before a better constitution is prepared to put in its place, it would also be truly absurd that such a fault be immediately and violently repaired. However, it can be required of those in power that they at least take to heart the maxim that such changes are necessary so as continuously to approach the goal (of the constitution most in accord with the laws of right). A nation may already possess republican rule, even if under its present constitution it has a despotic *ruling power*, until gradually the people are capable of being influenced by the mere idea of the law's authority (just as if it possessed physical power) and thus is found able to be its own legislator (which [ability] is originally based on [natural] right). If—through a violent *revolution* caused by a bad constitution—a constitution conforming to law were introduced by illegal means, it must not be permissible to lead the people back to the old one, even though everyone who violently or covertly participated in the revolution would rightly have been subject to the punishment due rebels. But as to the external relations among nations, it cannot be expected that a nation will give up its constitution, even if despotic (which is the stronger in relation to foreign enemies), so long as it risks the danger of being overrun by other nations; consequently, it is permissible to delay the intention to implement improvements until a better opportunity arises.*

373

*These are permissive laws of reason: To allow a condition of public right afflicted with injustice to continue until everything is either of itself or through peaceful means ripe for a complete transformation, for any *legal* constitution, even if it conforms with right only to a small degree, is better than none, and the latter fate (anarchy) would result from *premature* reform. Political wisdom, therefore, will make it a duty, given the present state of things, to evaluate reforms against the ideal of public right. Revolutions brought about by nature itself will not find excuses for still greater oppression, but will use revolution as nature's call to create a lawful constitution based on principles of freedom, for only this fundamental reform is enduring.

It may be that despotic moralists (those who fail in practice) violate rules of political prudence in many ways (by adopting or proposing premature measures); still, experience will gradually bring them to give up their opposition to nature and to follow a better course. By contrast with this, the moralizing politician attempts, on the pretext that human nature is not *capable* of attaining the good as prescribed in the idea of reason, to extenuate political principles that are contrary to right, and thus these principles make progress *impossible* and perpetuate the violation of right.

Instead of employing the practical science that these politically prudent men make so much of, they use devious *practices* to influence the current ruling power (so as to insure their own private advantage), even at the expense of the people and, where possible, the entire world, acting just like lawyers (for whom law is a *trade*, not a matter of *legislation*) when they go into politics. For since it is not their business to be overly concerned with legislation, but rather to carry out momentary commands under the law of the land, they must always regard every existing legal constitution as best—and when it is amended in higher places, they regard these amendments as for the best, too; in that way, everything follows in its proper mechanical order. But, granted that this deftness at being all things to all men gives the politically prudent the illusion of being able to judge a *national constitution* in general against concepts of right (consequently, *a priori*, not empirically); and granted that they make a great to do of knowing *men* (which is certainly to be expected, since they deal with so many of them), though without knowing *man* and what can be made of him (for which a high standpoint of anthropological observation is required); nonetheless, if, as reason prescribes, they attempt to use these concepts in civil and international law, they cannot make the transition except in a spirit of charlatanism. For they will continue to follow their customary procedure (of mechanically applying despotically imposed laws of coercion) in an area where the concepts of reason only permit lawful compulsion that accords with principles of freedom, and it is under such principles alone that a rightful and enduring constitution is possible. The supposed practical man believes he can ignore the idea of right and solve this problem empirically, the solution being based on his experience of the national constitutions that have heretofore been most lasting, though oftentimes contrary to right. The maxims that he uses to this end (though he does not make them public) consist, roughly speaking, of the following sophistries.

374

1. *Fac et excusa.*[23] Seize every favorable opportunity for arbitrary usurpation (of a right of a nation either over its own people or over another neighboring people); the justification can be presented far more easily and elegantly *after the fact*, and the violence more easily glossed over (especially in the first case, where the supreme internal power is also the legislative authority, which one must obey without argument), than if one first thinks out convincing reasons and waits for objections to them. This audacity itself gives a certain appearance of an inner conviction that the act is right, and after the fact the god of success, *bonus eventus*, is the best advocate.

2. *Si fecisti, nega.*[24] Whatever crime you have committed—e.g., that you have reduced your people to despair and hence brought them to rebellion—deny that the guilt is *yours*; instead, maintain that it is the obstinacy of the subjects, or, if you have conquered a neighboring people, that the guilt belongs to human nature, for if one does not forestall others by using force, one can surely count on their anticipating it and becoming one's conqueror.   375

3. *Divide et impera.*[25] That is, if there are certain privileged persons among your people who have merely chosen you to be their leader *(primus inter pares)*,[26] destroy their unity and separate them from the people; and if, in turn, the people have delusions of greater freedom, everyone will depend on your unchecked will. Or if you are concerned with foreign nations, then sowing discord among them is a relatively certain method of subjecting them one after another to your will, all the while appearing to defend the weaker.

Certainly no one will be taken in by these political maxims, for all of them are widely known; nor are men ashamed of them, as if their injustice were altogether too apparent. For great powers never heed the judgment of the masses, feeling shame only in the face of others like them; and as regards the foregoing principles, not their becoming public knowledge, but only their *failure* can make those powers feel ashamed (for among themselves they agree on the morality of the maxims). And in this way their *political* honor, on which they can always count, is retained, namely, by the expansion of their power by whatever means they choose.*

---

*Although we might doubt the existence of a certain inherent wickedness in *men* who live together within a nation, and instead might plausibly point to

From all these twistings and turnings of an immoral doctrine of prudence regarding how men are to be brought out of the warlike state of nature into the state of peace, we receive at least this much illu-
376   mination: Men can no more escape the concept of right in their private relations than in their public ones; nor can they properly risk basing their politics on the handiwork of prudence alone, and, consequently, they cannot altogether refuse obedience to the concept of public right (which is particularly important in the case of international right). Instead, they give this concept all due honor, even if they also invent a hundred excuses and evasions to avoid observing it in practice, attributing to cunning force the authority that is the original source and bond of right. In order to end this sophistry (if not the injustice that it glosses over) and to force the false representatives of those in earthly power to confess that rather than right it is might that they advocate—a fact that is clear from the tone they adopt, as if they were entitled to give orders—it will do well to expose the fraud to which they subject themselves and others and to reveal the highest principle from which perpetual peace as an end

---

the lack of a sufficiently advanced culture (barbarism) as the cause of the unlawful aspects of their way of thinking, this wickedness is still completely and incontrovertibly apparent in foreign relations among *nations*. Within each nation this wickedness is concealed by the coercive power of civil law, for the citizens' inclination toward violence aginst one another is counteracted by a greater power, namely, that of the government. Not only does this provide a veneer of morality (*causae non causae*), but by placing these inclinations toward outbreaks of lawlessness behind bars, it also actually makes it easier to
376   develop the moral capacity for direct and immediate respect for the law. Everyone believes of himself that he would truly venerate and abide by the concept of right, if only he could expect the same from everyone else, which it is government's part to insure; and by this means a large step towards morality is taken (although it is still not a moral step)—a large step towards willing the concept of duty for its own sake, without regard for any reciprocity. But since all persons have a good opinion of themselves but presuppose evil intentions in everyone else, they mutually have this opinion of one another, that they are all in point of *fact*, of little worth (though how this might be remains inexplicable, since it cannot be blamed on the *nature* of man as a free being). Since, however, respect for the concept of right, which no man is capable of denying, provides the most solemn sanction for the theory that man has the ability to act according to it, everyone sees that for one's own part one must act in accord with it, no matter how others may act.

proceeds. We will show that all the evil that stands in the way of perpetual peace derives from the fact that the political moralist begins
where the moral politician rightly stops; and, since the former sub-
ordinates his principles to his ends (i.e., puts the cart before the
horse), he defeats his own purpose of effecting an agreement
between politics and morals.

In order to bring practical philosophy into harmony with itself, it
is first necessary to resolve this question: In problems of practical
reason, must we begin from *material principles*, the end (as object
of the will), or from its *formal* one, i.e., the one (which rests only on
freedom in external relations) that is expressed thus: "Act so that you
can will that your maxim ought to become a universal law (no matter what the end may be)"?

377

Without doubt the latter principle must take precedence,
because as a principle of right it has unconditioned necessity,
whereas the former is necessary only if one assumes the existence of
those empirical conditions through which the proposed end can be
realized. And if this end (e.g., perpetual peace) were also a duty, it
must itself be derived from the formal principle of external action.
Now the first principle, that of the *political moralists* (concerning
the problem of civil, international and cosmopolitan right), proposes a mere *technical task (problema technicum)*; by contrast, the second is the principle of the *moral politician*, for whom it is a *moral
task (problema morale)*, and its method of pursuing perpetual
peace—which one now desires not merely as a physical good, but
also as a condition that arises from acknowledging one's duty—is
completely distinct.

Solving the first problem, namely, the problem that political prudence proposes, requires considerable natural knowledge so that
one can use nature's mechanism to attain the desired end; yet it is
uncertain how this mechanism will function as far as its consequences for perpetual peace are concerned; and this is so in all
three areas of public right. Whether the people's obedience and
prosperity will be better preserved over a long period of time by
harshness or by appeals to vanity, by granting supreme power to a
single ruler or to several united ones, or, perhaps, merely by a devoted aristocracy or by the power of the people is uncertain. History
furnishes examples of the opposite effects being produced by all
forms of government (with the singular exception of true republicanism, which alone can appeal to the sensibility of a moral politi-

cian). Still more uncertainty arises in the area of *international right*—a form of right purportedly based on statutes worked out by ministers—for in fact it is a term without content, and it rests on contracts whose very act of conclusion contains the secret reservation for their violation. By contrast, the solution to the second problem, the problem of *political wisdom*, impresses itself on us, as it were, for it obviously puts all artificiality to shame, and leads directly to the end. Yet prudence cautions us not to employ power in direct pursuit of it, but rather to approach it indirectly through those conditions presented by favorable circumstances.

378

Thus, it may be said: "Seek first the kingdom of pure practical reason and its *righteousness*, and your end (the blessing of perpetual peace) will come to you of itself."[27] For this characteristic is inherent in morals—especially as regards its fundamental principle of public right (consequently, in relation to a politics that is *a priori* knowable)—that the less it makes conduct depend on the proposed end, be it a physical or moral advantage, the more conduct will in general harmonize with morality. And this is because such conduct derives directly from the general will that is given *a priori* (in a single people or in the relations of different peoples to one another), which alone determines what is right among men. If only it is acted on in a consistent way, this unity of the will of all can, along with the mechanism of nature, be the cause of the desired result and can make the concept of right effective. So, for example, it is a fundamental principle of moral politics that in uniting itself into a nation a people ought to subscribe to freedom and equality as the sole constituents of its concept of right, and this is not a principle of prudence, but is founded on duty. By contrast, political moralists do not even deserve a hearing, no matter how much they argue that the natural mechanism of a group of people who enter into society invalidates that fundamental principle and vitiates its intention, or seek to substantiate their contentions by use of ancient and modern examples of badly organized constitutions (e.g., of democracies without systems of representation). This is especially so since such a damaging theory may bring about the evil that it prophesies, for in it man is thrown into the same class as other living machines, which need only to become conscious that they are not free in order to become in their own eyes the most wretched of all the earth's creatures.

The true, albeit somewhat boastful proverb, *Fiat iustia, pereat mundus*—"Let justice reign, even if all the rogues in the world

should perish"—is a sound principle of right that cuts across the   379
sinuous paths of deceit and power. But it must not be misunder-
stood nor, perhaps, taken as permission simply to press with the
utmost vigour for one's own right (for that would conflict with
moral duty); instead, those in power should understand it to pose
an obligation not to deny or diminish anyone's rights through either
dislike or sympathy. Above all, this requires that the nation have an
internal constitution founded on principles of right and that it also
unite itself (analogously to a universal nation) with other neighboring and distant nations so they can settle their differences legally.
This proposition means only that adherence to political maxims
must not be based on the benefit or happiness that each nation
anticipates from so doing—thus, not on the end that each nation
makes an object (of its desire) and its supreme (though empirical)
principle of political wisdom; instead, adherence must derive from
the pure concept of the duty of right (from the *ought*, whose principle is given *a priori* through pure reason), let the physical consequences be what they may. The world will certainly not cease to
exist if there are fewer bad men. The intrinsic characteristic of
moral evil is that its aims (especially in relation to other like-mind-
ed persons) are self-contradictory and self-destructive, and it thus
makes way for the (moral) principle of goodness, even if progress in
doing so is slow.

Objectively (i.e., in theory) there is utterly no conflict between
morality and politics. But subjectively (in the self-seeking inclinations of men, which, because they are not based on maxims of reason, must not be called the [sphere of] practice) this conflict will
always remain, as well it should; for it serves as the whetstone of
virtue, whose true courage (according to the principle, *"tu ne cede
malis, sed contra audentior ito"*)[28] in the present case consists not so
much in resolutely standing up to the evils and sacrifices that must
be taken on; rather, it consists in detecting, squarely facing, and
conquering the deceit of the evil principle in ourselves, which is the
more dangerously devious and treacherous because it excuses all
our transgressions with an appeal to human nature's frailty.

In fact, the political moralist can say that the ruler and the peo-   380
ple, or the people and the people, do not treat *one another* wrong

if, through violence and fraud they war against one another, although they do in general act wrong when they deny respect to the concept of right, on which alone peace can be perpetually based. When one person violates the rights of another who is just as lawlessly disposed towards him, then whatever *happens* to them as they destroy themselves is entirely right; enough of their race will always survive so that this game will not cease, even into the remotest age, and they can serve as a warning to later generations. In this manner, the course of world events justifies providence. For the moral principle in man never dies out, and with the continuous progress of culture, reason, which is able pragmatically to apply the ideas of right in accordance with the moral principle, grows through its persistence in doing so, and guilt for transgressions grows concomitantly. (Given that the human race never can and never will be in a better condition) it seems impossible to be able to use a theodicy to provide any justification whatsoever for creation, namely, that such a race of generally corrupt beings should have been put on earth. We will be unavoidably driven to such skeptical conclusions, if we do not assume that pure principles of right have objective reality, i.e., that they permit themselves to be applied and that peoples in nations and even nations in their relations with one another must for their parts behave in conformity with them, no matter how objectionable empirical politics may find them. Thus, true politics cannot progress without paying homage to morality; and although politics by itself is a difficult art, its union with morality is not art at all, for this union cuts through the [Gordian] knot that politics cannot solve when politics and morality come into conflict. The rights of men must be held sacred, however great the cost of sacrifice may be to those in power. Here one cannot go halfway, cooking up hybrid, pragmatically-conditioned rights (which are somewhere between the right and the expedient); instead, all politics must bend its knee before morality, and by so doing it can hope to reach, though but gradually, the stage where it will shine in light perpetual.

II

On the Agreement between Politics and Morality under the
Transcendental Concept of Public Right

If, in thinking about public right as jurists customarily do, I abstract
from its *matter* (i.e., the different empirically given relations among
men in a nation or among nations), the *form of publicity*, whose possibility every claim of right intrinsically contains, still remains, and
unless every such claim has this form there can be no justice (that
can be regarded as *publicly knowable*), thus no right either, since
the right can be conferred only through justice. Every claim of right
must have this capacity for publicity, and since one can easily judge
whether or not it is present in a particular case, i.e., whether or not
publicity is compatible with the agent's principles, it provides us
with a readily applicable criterion that is found *a priori* in reason;
for the purported claim's *(praetensio iuris)* falseness (contrariness to
right) is immediately recognized by an experiment of pure reason.

Having abstracted in this way from everything empirical contained in the concept of national and international right (such as
the wickedness in human nature that makes coercion necessary),
one can call the following proposition the *transcendental formula* of
public right:

"All actions that affect the rights of other men are wrong if
their maxim is not consistent with publicity."

This principle is to be considered not only *ethical* (as belonging
to the doctrine of virtue), but also *juridical* (as pertaining to the
rights of men). If my maxim cannot be *openly divulged* without at
the same time defeating my own intention, i.e., must be kept *secret*
for it to succeed, or if I cannot *publicly acknowledge* it without
thereby inevitably arousing everyone's opposition to my plan, then
this necessary and universal, and thus *a priori* foreseeable, opposition of all to me could not have come from anything other than the
injustice with which it threatens everyone. Further, it is merely *negative*, i.e., it serves only as a means for recognizing what is *not right* 382
in regard to others. Like any axiom, it is seen in the following examples of public right.

1. In regard to *civil right (ius civitas)*, namely, rights internal to a
nation, the following question arises, one that many believe is diffi-

cult to answer, but that the transcendental principle of publicity solves with utter ease: "May a people rightfully use rebellion to over-throw the oppressive power of a so-called tyrant *(nontitulo, sed exercitio talis)*?" The rights of the people are injured, and no injustice comes to him (the tyrant) who is deposed, of that there is no doubt. Nonetheless, it remains wrong in the highest degree for the subjects to pursue their rights in this way, and they can in no way complain of injustice if they are defeated in this conflict and must subsequently suffer the harshest punishment for it.

A great many arguments can be offered on both sides when one attempts to settle this issue by a dogmatic deduction of the foundations of right. Only the transcendental principle of the publicity of public right will spare us this long-windedness. According to this principle, before establishing the social contract, the people have to ask whether it dare make known the maxim of its intention to revolt in some circumstances. One can readily see, first, that if one were to make revolt a condition of the establishment of a nation's constitution that force might then in certain circumstances be used against the ruler and, second, that the people must in such an instance claim some rightful power over the ruler. In that case, he would not be the ruler; or if as a condition of establishing the nation, both the people and the ruler were given power, there would be no possibility whatsoever of doing what it was the people's intention to do. The wrongness of revolt revealed by the fact that the maxim through which one *publicly declares it* renders one's own intention impossible. One must therefore necessarily keep it secret. This secrecy, however, is not necessary on the part of the nation's ruler. He can say quite openly that he will punish with death the ringleader of every rebellion, even if they believe that he has been the first to transgress the fundamental law. For if he knows that he possesses *irresistibly* supreme power (which must be assumed in every civil constitution, since he who lacks sufficient might to protect each of his people against every other, also does not have the right to give orders), he does not have to worry that his own intention will be defeated if his maxim becomes known. It is perfectly consistent with this view that if the people's revolt succeeds, the ruler, returning to the status of a subject, cannot begin a new revolt to return himself to power, nor should he have to fear being called to account for his previous administration of the nation.

2. *Concerning international right:* There can be talk of international right only on the assumption that a state of law-governedness exists (i.e., that external condition under which a right can actually be accorded man). For as a public right, its concept already contains the public recognition of a general will that determines the rights of everyone, and this *status iuridicus* must proceed from some contract that cannot be founded on coercive laws (like those from which the nation springs), but can at best be an *enduring free* association, like the federation of different nations mentioned above. For in the state of nature, in the absence of a state of law-governedness, only private right can exist. Here another conflict between politics and morality (considering the latter as a doctrine of right) arises, to which, however, the criterion of the publicity of maxims finds easy application, though only if the contract binds the nations for the sole purpose of maintaining peace among themselves and between them and other nations, and not with the intention of conquest. This introduces the following instances of antinomy between politics and morality, along with their solution.

(a) "If one of these nations has promised something to another, be it aid, cession of certain territories, or subsidies, and so on, it may be asked whether, in those cases where the nation's well-being is at stake, it can be released from its promise by maintaining that it must be considered to have two roles: first, that of a sovereign, who is answerable to no one in the nation; and, on the other hand, merely that of the highest *political official*, who must give an account of his actions to the nation. From this we draw the following conclusion, that what the nation had bound itself to by virtue of its first role, it frees itself from in its second." But if a nation (or its ruler) were to allow its maxim to be known, then all others would quite naturally either flee from it or would unite with others in order to   384
oppose its arrogance. This proves that, given all its cunning, politics would in this way (through openness) defeat its end; consequently, that maxim is wrong.

(b) "If a neighboring power grows so formidably great *(potentia tremenda)* as to cause anxiety, can one assume that it will want to oppress others because it *can*; and does this give the lesser powers a right to (unified) attack on it, even without previous injury?" A nation that *let it be known* that it affirmed this maxim would suffer evil even more certainly and quickly. For the greater power would beat the lesser ones to the punch, and, as far as concerns the union of the latter, that would only be a feeble reed against one who knew how to employ the maxim *divide et impera.*

(c) "If a smaller nation is so located that it divides some territory that a larger one regards as necessary to its preservation, is not the latter justified in subjugating the smaller one and incorporating it into itself?" One can easily see that the larger must not allow it to become known that it has adopted such a maxim; for either the smaller nations would unite very early, or other powers would fight over the prey, and, consequently, openness would render the maxim ineffectual, a sign that it is wrong, and, indeed, perhaps to a very high degree. For a small object of wrong [action] does not prevent the wrong done to it from being very great.

3. Here I silently pass over the issue of *cosmopolitan right,* for, given its analogy with international right, its maxims are easy to adduce and validate.

In the principle of the incompatibility between the maxims of international right and publicity one has a good indication of the *incommensurability* of politics and morality (as a doctrine of right). But one now needs also to become aware of the conditions under which the maxims of politics agree with the right of peoples. For it cannot be conversely concluded that whatever maxims are compatible with publicity are also for that reason right, for he who has decisively supreme power, has no need to keep his maxims secret. The condition underlying the possibility of international right in general is that there first exist a *state of right.* For without this there is no public right, and all right other than this (in the state of nature) that one can think of is merely private right. Now we have seen above that a federative state of nations whose only purpose is to prevent war is the only state of *right* compatible with their *freedom.* Thus, it is possible to make politics commensurable with morality only in a federative union (which is therefore necessary and given *a priori* in conformity with the principles of right); and the foundation of right underlying all political prudence is the establishment of this union to the greatest possible extent, for without this as an end all the sophistry of political prudence is contrary to wisdom, hence mere veiled wrong. The *casuistry* of this pseudopolitics is unsurpassed by the best of the Jesuit scholars, including as it does the *reservatio*

385

mentalis, i.e., formulating public contracts in such terms (e.g., the distinction between a *status quo* of *fact* and of *right*) that, whatever the occasion, one can interpret them in one's own favor; including, further, the *probabilismus,* i.e., attributing evil intentions to others, or making the likelihood of their possible superior power into a justification of the right to undercut other, peaceful nations; and, finally, the *peccatum philosophicum (peccatillum, baggatelle),* i.e., maintaining it to be an easily dismissible triviality to devour a *small* nation when some purportedly very much *greater* benefit to the world is a result.*

Politics' duplicitous relation to morality by first using one of its branches and then the other in pursuit of its purposes is fed by this casuistry. Both the love of man and the respect for the rights of man are our duty; the former is only *conditional,* while the latter is an *unconditional,* absolutely imperative duty, a duty that one must be completely certain of not having transgressed, if one is to be able to enjoy the sweet sense of having done right. Politics readily agrees with morality in the first sense (as ethics) for both surrender men's rights to their rulers. But with regard to morality in the second sense (as doctrine of right), before which it must bend the knee, politics finds it advisable not to enter into any relation whatsoever and, unfortunately, denies all reality to morality and reduces all duties to mere benevolence. This ruse of a secretive politics could be easily defeated were philosophy to give publicity to the maxims of politics, if politicians would only allow philosophers to give publicity to their own.

386

With this in mind, I propose another transcendental and affirmative principle of right, whose formula is:

"All maxims that *require* publicity (in order not to fail of their end) agree with both politics and morality."

*Documentation for such maxims can be found in Counselor Garve's treatise *"Über die Verbindung der Moral mit der Politik,"* [*On the Unity of Morality and Politics*], 1788.[29] This worthy scholar admits at the outset that he is unable to give an adequate answer to this question. But to approve of this union while granting that one cannot fully meet the objections that can be brought against it seems to be more forebearing than is advisable toward those who will most tend to misuse it.

For if they can achieve their end only through publicity, they must also conform to the universal public end (happiness), and it is the singular task of politics to establish this (to make the public satisfied with its state). But if this end can be attained only by publicity, i.e., by removing all mistrust of the maxims through which it is to be achieved, these maxims must harmonize with public right, for in this latter alone is the unity of all ends possible. I must postpone the further development and explanation of this principle for another occasion. But that it is a transcendental formula can be seen from the absence of all empirical conditions (of the doctrine of happiness), as material of the law, and from the reference it makes to the mere form of universal lawfulness.

If it is a duty to make the state of public right actual, though only through an unending process of approximation to it, and if at the same time there is a well founded hope that we can do it, then *perpetual peace*, which will follow the hitherto falsely so-called treaties of peace (but which are really only suspension of war), is no empty idea, but a task that, gradually completed, steadily approaches its goal (since the times during which equal progress occurs will, we hope, become ever shorter).

Translator Notes to To Perpetual Peace

1. *Kant's gesammelte Schriften,* hrsg. Königliche Preussische Akademie der Wissenschaften, Walter de Gruyter & Co., Berlin and Leipzig, 1904–, Bd. VIII, pp. 341–86. This is the standard reference edition for Kant's work. The numbers in the margins refer to the page numbers in this volume. *Perpetual Peace* was first published in 1795 in Königsberg by Friedrich Nicolovius. A second, enlarged edition appeared in 1796. The specific occasion for which Kant wrote the essay is unknown, but speculation is that he was moved to do so by the signing of the Treaty of Basel on April 5, 1795.

Kant's footnotes are indicated by an asterisk, *. The translator's footnotes are indicated by superscript numbers.

2. I have translated the German term *Staat* by the English term "nation," even though the cognate "state" initially seems more natural. This decision is based on three considerations. First, what we think of as a nation, governed under a common constitution, in fact more closely corresponds to Kant's use of *Staat*, than does the present common usage of "state," particularly in the United States. Second, Kant uses *Zustand* when he refers to the state of nature and the law-governed state. Using "state" for *Zustand* better conforms with the tradition of English usage going back to Hobbes, than *Zustand* as "condition." Finally, using "state" to render both *Staat* and *Zustand* would have resulted in confusion.

3. Reichsgraf Joseph Niklaus Windisch-Graetz (1744–1802) proposed a prize question regarding the formulation of contracts in such a way that they could have only a single interpretation, thereby eliminating disputes over the transfer of property.

4. Kant's conception of the state of nature is clearly similar to Hobbes'. Kant would have been able to read either *De Cive*, where the state of nature is discussed in chapter 1, section 12, or the Latin version of *Leviathan*, where the relevant discussion is in chapter 13, as in the original English version.

5. In some slight contrast to the translation tradition, I render *das Recht* (and *das Unrecht*), as well as their adjectival forms, as "right" (and "wrong"), rather than "just" (and "unjust"). Where Kant uses these terms in reference to political theory and legality, their conceptual content derives from the context of morality, where these term denote a moral property of actions, a property Kant argues can be isolated by using the Categorical Imperative in formulating maxims for our actions. One of Kant's primary claims in *Perpetual Peace* is that consideration of rightness and wrongness ought to permeate human action in every sphere, taking

precedence over all others, and I thus chose terms that for most of us denote moral properties of actions.

6. Frederick II (The Great) of Prussia.

7. Jacques Mallet du Pan (1749–1800) in *Über die französische Revlution and die Ursachen irer Dauer* (1794) *(On the French Revolution and the Causes of Its Duration)*. Du Pan was a Swiss-born opponent of the revolution.

8. Alexander Pope, *Essay on Man* III, 303–4.

9. H. Grotius (1583–1645), *De jure belli et pacis*, 1625; Samuel von Pufendorf (1632–1694), *De jure naturae et gentium*, 1672; Emer de Vattel (1714–1767), *Le droit des gens*, 1758.

10. "And godless Furor shall sit/Inside on his frightful weapons, hands bound with a hundred/Brass knots behind him, and roar with bloody mouth. Vergil, *Aeneid* I, 294–6 (Lind translation).

11. "every need/pours from the lap of earth and magic nature." Lucretius, *The Nature of Things*, V, 233–4 (Copley translation).

12. *Zweck* and *Zweckmässigkeit* have given all of Kant's translators problems. I have chosen "end" as my primary English translation for *Zweck*, though I sometimes use "goal." Both connote the consequence or result that one intends to achieve by adopting a particular plan and pursuing a specific course of action, and these are at the heart of Kant's use of the term. For *Zweckmässigkeit*, however, I use "puposiveness," which is a traditional rendering that comes close to capturing Kant's sense. The problem with this solution, of course, is that it fails to preserve graphically the linguistic relationship between the two terms.

13. "Providence conditions; once she commands, they always obey."

14. "griffins may yet mate with mares." Vergil, *Eclogues*, VIII, 27 (Lewis translation).

15. A single cause suffices.

16. This and the following discussion turns on Kant's distinction between the dogmatically theoretical and morally practical perspectives. The dogmatically theoretical perspective is the one from which we finite creatures can properly speak of having cognitive knowledge. Such knowledge involves *both* a sensory *and* a conceptual element. Without both, Kant argues in the *Critique of Pure Reason*, what we tend to think of as demonstrably true scientific knowledge is not possible. On the other hand, there are some matters of vital interest to creatures such as ourselves about which,

though we can have no knowledge of the forgoing type, we must necessarily have beliefs. Specifically, we all do have beliefs about freedom, immortality, and God, and these are matters that Kant argues we can consider only from the morally practical perspective. His view, then, is that we cannot have dogmatically theoretical knowledge of their existence and nature, but from the morally practical perspective we are justified in having beliefs about them. See the *Critique of Pure Reason*, A633/B661-A636?B664 and A797/B825-A819?B847; see also the *Critique of Judgment*, 179–86.

17. "The fates lead him who is willing, but drag him who is unwilling." Seneca, *Epist. Mor.* XVIII, 4.

18. Friedrich Bouterwek (1766–1828).

19. Woe to the vanquished.

20. Kant's reference here is to the organization of the German university at the time, which consisted of three "higher" (graduate) faculties of Theology, Law, and Medicine, and a "lower" (undergraduate) faculty of Philosophy. His view, expressed in *The Contest of the Faculties*, is that although the three "higher" faculties might properly be subject to control by the government, since they train persons to perform in areas of specific concern to the government, the "lower" faculty educates persons as persons and should therefore be free of both government control and control by the "higher" faculties.

21. Beyond possibility there is no obligation.

22. Matt. 10:16.

23. Act first, then justify.

24. If you are the perpetrator, deny it.

25. Divide and conquer.

26. First among equals.

27. Matt. 6:33.

28. "do not yield to misfortune, but press on more boldly/Than your fortune allows you." Vergil, *Aeneid*, VI, 95 (Lind translation).

29. Christian Garve (1742–1798), *Abhandlung über die Verbindung der Moral mit der Politik oder einige Betrachtungen uber de Frage, inweifern es mögliche sei, die Moral des Privatlebens bei der Regierung der Staaten zu beobachten* (Breslau, 1788) *(Treatise on the Connection of Morality with Politics, or Some Questions on the Extent to Which It Is Possible for the Governments of Nations to Observe Morality in Private Lives).*

Bibliography

A. Writings by Kant

1. German

Kant, Immanuel. *Kant's gesammelte Schriften*, 28 vols. Berlin and Leipzig: Walter de Gruyter & Co., 1904–.

2. English

Kant, Immanuel. *Critique of Judgment*, trans. Werner S. Pluhar. Indianapolis: Hackett Publishing Company, 1987.

———. *Critique of Practical Reason*, trans. Werner S. Pluhar. Indianapolis: Hackett Publishing Company, 2002.

———. *Critique of Pure Reason*, trans. Werner S. Pluhar. Indianapolis: Hackett Publishing Company, 1996.

———. *Grounding for the Metaphysics of Morals*, trans. James W. Ellington. Indianapolis: Hackett Publishing Company, 1981.

———. *Metaphysical Elements of Justice*, 2nd ed., trans. John Ladd. Indianapolis: Hackett Publishing Company, 1999.

———. *Metaphysical Principles of Virtue*, trans. James Ellington. Indianapolis: Hackett Publishing Company, 1982.

———. *Perpetual Peace and Other Essays on Politics, History, and Morals*, trans. Ted Humphrey. Indianapolis: Hackett Publishing Company, 1983.

B. Writings on Kant

1. Selected General Books on Kant's Philosophy

Beck, Lewis While. *Early German Philosophy*. Cambridge, MA: Harvard University Press, 1969. Chapter XVII.

Cassirer, Ernst. *Kant's Life and Thought*, trans. James Haden. New Haven: Yale University Press, 1981.

Höffe, Otfried. *Immanuel Kant*, trans. Marshall Farrier. Albany: State University of New York Press, 1994.

Keuhn, Manfred. *Kant: A Biography*. Cambridge, Cambridge University Press, 2001.

Walker, Ralph C. S. *Kant*. London: Routledge & Kegan Paul, 1978.

2. *Selected Books and Articles Concerned with Kant's Moral and Political Theory and Philosophy of History*

Allison, Henry E. *Kant's Theory of Freedom*. Cambridge: Cambridge University Press, 1990.

Axinn, Sidney. "Kant on World Government," in Gerhard Funke and Thomas M. Seebohm, eds., *Proceedings of the Sixth International Kant Congress*. Two Volumes. Washington, DC: University Press of America, 1989.

Bartleson, Jens. "The Trial of Judgment: A Note on Kant and the Paradoxes of Internationalism." *International Studies Quarterly* 39 (June 1995): 255–80.

Bohman, James and Lutz-Bachmann, Matthias, eds. *Perpetual Peace: Essays on Kant's Cosmopolitan Ideal*. Boston: MIT Press, 1997.

Bok, Sissela. *A Strategy for Peace: Human Values and the Threat of War*. New York: Pantheon Books, 1989.

Boucher, David. *Political Theories of International Relations*. Oxford: Oxford University Press, 1998.

Byrd, Sharon. "Perpetual Peace: A 20th Century Project" in Hoke Robinson, ed., *Proceedings of the Eighth International Kant Congress*. Two Volumes. Milwaukee: Marquette University Press, 1995: 343–57.

———. "The State as a 'Moral Person,'" in Hoke Robinson, ed., *Proceedings of the Eighth International Kant Congress*. Two Volumes. Milwaukee: Marquette University Press, 1995: 171–89.

Cavallar, Georg. "Kant's Society of Nations: Free Federation or World Republic?" *Journal of the History of Philosophy* 32 (July 1994): 461–82.

Covell, Charles. *Kant and the Law of Peace: A Study in the Philosophy of International Law and International Relations*. London: Macmillan Press Ltd., 1998.

————. *Kant, Liberalism and the Pursuit of Justice in the International Order*. Studies in the History of International Relations. Band 1. Münster, 1994.

Despland, Michel. *Kant on History and Religion*, with a translation of Kant's "On the Failure of All Attempted Philosophical Theodicies." Montreal and London: McGill-Queen's University Press, 1973.

Galston, William A. *Kant and the Problem of History*. Chicago and London: The University of Chicago Press, 1975.

Geismann, Georg. "On the Philosophically Unique Realism of Kant's Doctrine of Eternal Peace," in Hoke Robinson, ed., *Proceedings of the Eighth International Kant Congress*. Two Volumes. Milwaukee: Marquette University Press, 1995: 273–89

Huntley, Wade L. "Kant's Third Image: Systemic Sources of the Liberal Peace." *International Studies Quarterly* 40 (1996): 45–76.

Hutchings, Kimberly. *Kant, Critique, and Politics*. New York: Routledge, 1996

Kersting, Wolfgang. "Politics, Freedom, and Order: Kant's Political Philosophy," trans. Paul Guyer, in Paul Guyer, ed., *The Cambridge Companion to Kant*. Cambridge: Cambridge University Press, 1992.

Layne, C. "Kant or Cant: The Myth of the Democratic Peace." *International Security* 19 (1994): 5–49.

Lynch, Cecilia. "Kant, the Republican Peace, and Moral Guidance in International Law." *Ethics and International Affairs* 8 (1994): 39–58.

McFarland, J. D. *Kant's Concept of Teleology*. Edinburgh: The University Press, 1970.

Mertens, Thomas. "Cosmopolitanism and Citizenship: Kant Against Habermas." *European Journal of Philosophy* 4 (December 1996): 328–47.

Mulholland, Leslie A. "Kant on War and International Justice." *Kant-Studien* 78 (1987): 25–41.

————. *Kant's System of Rights*. New York: Columbia University Press, 1996.

Negretto, Gabriel L. "Kant and the Illusion of Collective Security." *Journal of International Affairs* 46 (Winter 1993): 501–24.

Pangle, Thomas L. and Ahrendorf, Peter J. *Justice Among Nations: On the Moral Basis of Power and Peace*. Lawrence: University Press of Kansas, 1999.

Raulet, G. "Citizenship, Otherness, and Cosmopolitanism in Kant." *Social Science Research* 35 (September 1996): 437–46.

Shell, Susan Meld. *The Rights of Reason: A Study of Kant's Philosophy and Politics.* Toronto, London, and Buffalo: University of Toronto Press, 1980.

Sullivan, Roger J. *Immanuel Kant's Moral Theory.* Cambridge: Cambridge University Press, 1989.

Teson, Fernando R. "The Kantian Theory of International Law." *Columbia Law Review* 92 (January 1992): 53–102.

Thompson, Kenneth W. *Fathers of International Thought: The Legacy of Political Theory.* Baton Rouge and London: Louisiana State University Press, 1994.

Van der Linden, Harry. "Kant: The Duty to Promote International Peace and Political Intervention," in Hoke Robinson, ed., *Proceedings of the Eighth International Kant Congress.* Two Volumes. Milwaukee: Marquette University Press, 1995: 71–79.

Walzer, Michael. *Just and Unjust Wars: A Moral Argument with Historical Illustrations.* New York: Basic Books, 1977.

Williams, Howard. *Kant's Political Philosophy.* New York: St. Martin's Press, 1983.

Williams, Howard and Booth, Ken. "Kant: Theorist beyond Limits," in Ian Clark and Iver B. Neumann, eds., *Classical Theories of International Relations.* London: Macmillan Press, 1996: 71–98.

Williams, Michael C. "Reason and Realpolitik: Kant's Critique of International Politics." *Canadian Journal of Political Science* 25 (March 1992): 99–119.

Wood, Allen W. "Kant's Project of Perpetual Peace," in Hoke Robinson, ed., *Proceedings of the Eighth International Kant Congress.* Two Volumes. Milwaukee: Marquette University Press, 1995: 3–18.

Yovel, Yirmiaha. *Kant and the Philosophy of History.* Princeton, NJ: Princeton University Press, 1980.